Transcending Divorce

Also by Alan Wolfelt

*Healing A Child's Grieving Heart: 100 Practical Ideas
for Families, Friends & Caregivers*

*Healing A Friend's Grieving Heart: 100 Practical Ideas
for Helping Someone You Love Through Loss*

*Healing A Teen's Grieving Heart: 100 Practical Ideas for
Families, Friends & Caregivers*

Healing Your Grieving Heart: 100 Practical Ideas

The Journey Through Grief: Reflections on Healing

*Living in the Shadow of the Ghosts of Grief:
Step Into the Light*

*The Transcending Divorce Journal:
Exploring the Ten Essential Touchstones*

*The Transcending Divorce Support Group Guide:
Guidance and Meeting Plans for Facilitators*

The Wilderness of Divorce: Finding Your Way

Companion
P R E S S

Companion Press is dedicated to the education and support
of both the bereaved and bereavement caregivers. We believe
that those who companion the bereaved by walking with them
as they journey in grief have a wondrous opportunity: to help
others embrace and grow through grief—and to lead fuller, more
deeply-lived lives themselves because of this important ministry.

For a complete catalog and ordering information, write or call:

Companion Press
The Center for Loss and Life Transition
3735 Broken Bow Road
Fort Collins, Colorado 80526
(970) 226-6050

www.centerforloss.com

Transcending Divorce

Ten Essential Touchstones for Finding Hope and Healing Your Heart

Alan D. Wolfelt, Ph.D.

Companion
PRESS

Fort Collins, Colorado
An imprint of the Center for Loss and Life Transition

Companion Press is an imprint of the Center for Loss and Life Transition, 3735 Broken Bow Road, Fort Collins, Colorado 80526.

Printed in the United States of America.

17 16 15 14 13 12 11 10 09 08   5 4 3 2 1

ISBN: 978-1-879651-50-0

To the people who have invited me to walk with them through the wilderness of their divorce transitions. Thank you for transforming your pain into wisdom and your sadness into joy. What you have taught me I try to teach others. Thank you for entrusting me with your stories of love and loss.

Contents

Introduction and Welcome

"Divorce is a metaphorical surgery that affects all areas of your life."
Virginia Satir

Thank you for picking up *Transcending Divorce* and allowing me to companion you on your journey. I, too, have walked this path, and I understand that in your heart you have come to experience deep pain along the way. As you read and reflect on the contents of this book, I hope and pray that you realize you are not alone.

This book is a fulfillment of one of my life hopes: a gathering of some valuable Touchstones into a resource that I hope will make a difference in the lives of people who are walking where I have walked as a divorced person.

Very few relationships in our human experience are more significant than the relationship we call marriage. For this reason, few life experiences are more difficult than the ending of what was once an intimate relationship.

Even for those who seek the divorce, there is overwhelming loss—the loss of dreams, an ideal, an image and hopes that each partner had for this marriage in the beginning. Naturally, divorce impacts your sense of who you are, your beliefs about safety and security, as well as your understanding about love, relationships, family and commitment. Life as you have known it has been "torn apart," and now you have some "special needs" that demand and deserve your attention.

Without a doubt, relationships are one of the most important aspects of our lives. It is through relationships that we create our identities and discover who we are. With divorce comes the reality that the center around which you have defined yourself and your life is gone. Divorce creates an entirely different context for you and alters the way you view your past, present and future. As old routines are dramatically altered, you are faced with creating a new life. Yes, you are in uncharted territory.

Bringing to an end what you at one time thought would be a permanent fixture in your life naturally results in disorientation and confusion, anxiety and fear, loss and loneliness. Yes, divorce brings a multitude of emotions and responsibilities that may seem overwhelming. A new home may need to be created. Your finances may be difficult and stressful to manage. If you have children, they will naturally

An invitation to all whose significant relationships have ended

Please know that whether you were officially and legally married or part of a committed nontraditional love relationship that is ending, this book is for you. The word divorce means "separation." If you are separating from a partner, whether you were married, living together or simply a "couple," the end of your love relationship is essentially a divorce. Married or unmarried, you have the same needs to mourn the lost relationship and journey through the wilderness of your grief. I invite you to use this book to help you achieve integration of your grief.

have difficult questions. They may be depressed, feel angry and act-out their grief at a time when you do not feel equipped to help them. You may feel alone or emptied out. You may feel as if you are not only losing your marriage but also yourself. You may struggle with knowing who you are and wonder how you will survive this major life change. You may question what your future holds.

If you relate to any of this, you are not overreacting to the pain of divorce. It is real and it is BIG!

Because of the overwhelming changes that divorce brings, it is so important to realize that moving forward will take time and hard work. Actually it will involve time and energy to do *grief* work! Grief work means that you have to mourn what you have lost before you can go forward. It will require that you are patient with yourself as you explore your old life and slowly work to create a new life. While this is naturally draining and challenging, the good news is that it is possible, and, *you are not alone*. Millions of people have experienced divorce and survived, and so will you!

With the awareness that divorce is a traumatic experience—one that impacts the very core of who you are psychologically and spiritually—comes the reality that in many ways your life will need to be rebuilt from the ground up. Ask yourself right now: Am I willing to be companioned on this difficult journey from what *was* to what *can be*? If your answer is yes, I welcome you to read on.

While my initial hope is to help you openly mourn your lost dreams and hopes, my ultimate goal is to help you develop a new vision of yourself and your future. I hope to companion you as you create a new life for yourself, one that allows you to feel alive, authentic, empowered and able to give and receive love openly in the future.

The Ten Touchstones

This brings us to the concept of the "Touchstones" that will help you in your journey. I have used the concept of Touchstones in this book because it speaks to my heart. By definition, a touchstone is a standard or norm against which to measure something. In this book I describe ten Touchstones, or benchmarks. These Touchstones are essential physical, emotional, cognitive, social, and spiritual *actions* for you to take if your hope is to integrate your divorce and to find renewed meaning and purpose in your life.

Think of the grief from your divorce as a wilderness—a vast, mountainous, inhospitable forest. You are in the midst of unfamiliar and often brutal surroundings. You are cold and tired. Yet, you must journey through this wilderness. To find your way out, you must become acquainted with its terrain and learn to follow the sometimes hard-to-find trail markers that lead to healing, restoration, and eventually, transcendence.

In the wilderness of your divorce grief, the Touchstones are your trail markers. They are the signs that you are on the right path. I also like to think of them as "wisdom teachings" that the many people I have companioned in their divorce journeys have conveyed to me. Of course, these Touchstones also became a lifeline in my own personal divorce experience.

Some soon-to-be and newly divorced people don't yet see that all the other survivors of ended marriages have left us many trail markers that show us how they made it through the wilderness. But they have. If we look, we will see that they have been gracious enough to pass them onto others who enter this inhospitable wilderness. Again, you are not alone. Others have gone before you and discovered the strength not only to survive, but eventually to thrive. From the depths of my being, I believe you can too!

When you learn to identify and make use of the Touchstones outlined in this book, you will not be as likely as you might otherwise to get lost in your divorce journey. However, even then the trail will often be arduous, and you may at times feel hopeless and confused. And even when you've become a master journeyer, and you know the terrain of your grief very well, you will sometimes feel like you are backtracking and being ravaged by the forces around you. This too is the nature of the grief that comes with divorce. Complete mastery of a wilderness experience is not possible. Just as we cannot control the winds and the storms and the beasts in nature, we can never have total dominion over our grief.

The Role of Surrender

My personal experience suggests that right when you are in the midst of your wilderness divorce experience, many well-meaning people will ask, "Why did you get a divorce?" While some people can respond to this question with clarity and deep insight, many of us find it difficult to answer clearly.

Sometimes we simply cannot completely understand the loss of our hoped-for relationship. We cannot totally understand it now, and we are not likely to ever understand it. Sometimes we can even still love someone but realize deep in our souls that we should not spend the rest of our lives with him or her. Maybe instead of thinking we need to totally understand or explain the "why" of our divorce, we need to allow ourselves to mourn the loss of what we hoped for in our marriage.

I have found that sometimes it is in staying open to the mystery and recognizing that we don't understand and can't control everything that some level of understanding comes. In fact, perhaps it is "standing-under" the mysterious experience of divorce that provides us with a unique perspective: We are not above or bigger than divorce. Maybe only after exhausting the search for understanding the "why" of our divorce can we discover a newly defined "why" for our own life.

In my experience, "understanding" comes when we *surrender*. That is, when we surrender our self-critical judgments (we need to be self-compassionate) and our need to completely understand (we never will). The grief that divorce brings has its own voice and should not be compromised by our need for judgment, or even complete understanding.

Impatience with ourselves and the expectation that we must completely understand the "why" of our divorce are perhaps the greatest enemies that hamper our capacity to surrender. Ironically, divorce requires patience and courage to let things fall apart, because that must happen before new growth can begin.

Be aware that surrender is not the same as resignation. Actually, surrendering to the unknowable mystery is a courageous choice, an act of faith, a trust in God and in yourself. Surrender can actually help you feel safe to mourn the loss of your relationship because there is nothing left to hide. Your growth begins when you realize you are facing parts of yourself and your situation that you need to face. Slow down and simmer. Breathe. Honor your own story. It's time to awaken. Remember, loss brings up anything that is hiding. Hold this mystery in your heart and surround yourself with caring, compassionate companions who sit with you in unconditional love, not in judgment of you or your journey.

So, I invite you to *surrender* to your work of mourning. For you see, if you become an intrepid traveler on your journey, if you make use of these ten Touchstones, I promise you that you will find your way out of the wilderness of your grief. You will learn to make the most of the precious life in front of you.

The Role of Hope

Hope is an equally important foundation of this book. Hope is an expectation of a good that is yet to be. It is an expression of the present alive with a sense of the possible. It is a belief that not only healing but transformation will occur.

Yes, this book will not only help you heal, it will help you experience transcendence. Thus, the title: *Transcending Divorce*. Transcendence, which literally means an entire change in form, goes beyond healing. In this context, divorce means to be altered, changed and modified. When you experience healing, you return to where you were before your injury (in other words, before your divorce). However, when you transcend, you can grow in any direction. To transcend from your divorce opens you up to new directions and positive changes to utilize your gifts in the world around you and to celebrate the richness and purpose of your life.

In honoring the ten Touchstones, you are making an effort to find hope for your continued life. Through intentional mourning of your marriage relationship, you yourself can be the purveyor of your hope. You create hope in yourself by actively mourning the death of your marriage and not only setting your intention to heal (see p. 19), but also to transcend.

When you feel frustrated and hopeless (and you no doubt will at times), you can also reach out to others for hope. Spend time in the company of people who affirm your need to mourn the loss of your marriage, yet, at the same time, give you hope for healing and transcendence.

People who are empathetic, nonjudgmental, good listeners and who model positive, optimistic ways of being in the world will be your best companions at this difficult time. They will help resupply you with hope when your stores are running low. They will help you build divine momentum toward your eventual exodus from the wilderness of your divorce grief.

Remember Your Heart

I insisted that the word "heart" be contained in the title of this book. Why? Because my learning from my own divorce experience, as well as the people who have trusted me to walk with them in their divorce experiences, have taught me that an open heart that is grieving is a "well of reception;" it is moved entirely by what it takes in or perceives. Authentic mourning of your lost relationship is an opportunity to embrace your open heart in ways that not only allow for healing, but encourage transcendence.

"The centerpiece of the integration of divorce is not the mind, but the heart."
A.D.W.

Perhaps the most important truth I have learned is that healing from divorce grief is heart-based, not head-based. Modern therapies sometimes separate the head from the heart; it's as if we should somehow be able to rationally think through our life losses. I *heartily* disagree! Carl Jung taught us years ago that every psychological struggle is ultimately a matter of spirituality. The contents of this book will encourage you to think, yes, but more importantly, to feel with your heart and soul.

Without doubt, if you allow yourself to, you will not only have thoughts but many heart-based feelings surrounding the upheaval that comes with divorce. As old routines

"We can only arrive at a new level of experience by means of a painful death of the soul, and what is more painful than the ending of a relationship?"
Thomas Moore

disappear, as well as some aspects of life you probably enjoyed at some point in the journey, you are left to create a new life. Many parts of your life change, and it is natural to experience anxiety and fear. The uncertainty of what your future holds can put you "at risk" for feeling paralyzed.

My hope is that you will remember that the antidote to fear is courage. The word courage comes from the Old French word for heart (*coeur*). Your courage grows for those things in life that impact you deeply. The experience of divorce opens, or engages, your heart. Now you must take your heart, which has been engaged, and muster the courage to encounter the ten essential Touchstones. Yes, this is a time to mobilize all the courage you can find within yourself.

Courage can also be defined as the ability to do what you believe is right, despite the fact that others may strongly and persuasively disagree. If this book helps you mourn the loss of your marriage, some people around you, even some family and friends, may try to shame you or tell you to "buck up" and "move forward." So, I remind you, go forth with courage and remember the affirmation, "I am not alone."

This book, directed from my heart to your heart, is an invitation to go to that spiritual place inside yourself and transcend a culture where many

"There are pains that cannot be contained in the mind—only in the heart."

Stephen Levine

people may directly or indirectly try to shame you for getting a divorce. Enter deeply into your journey. In many ways the path of the heart is an individual exploration into the wilderness, along unmarked and unlit paths. In part, my hope in this book is to provide you some light along your path.

Honoring Your Journey

I have attempted to convey in the following pages an "active empathy," encouraging you to be the expert regarding your own experience. You see, I have discovered a Touchstone in my own personal divorce journey and in my "companioning" of my fellow human beings like you. *I can only help people when I encourage them to teach me about their unique divorce experience.*

You may consider this helping attitude somewhat strange. After all, as a professional counselor, am I not supposed to "treat" the person who has come to me for help? No, not really. My experience has made me aware that thinking a trained counselor like myself should have all the answers for people experiencing divorce only complicates their experience. I prefer the use of a "companioning" or "teach me" attitude with my fellow travelers in this journey.

In sum, I have discovered that if I allow you to be my teacher, I not only become more helpful to you, but I am enriched in my own life. Likewise, if you as the person experiencing divorce transition conceive of yourself as the expert of your own journey, you will feel empowered to own what you are feeling and not feel shamed by the sometimes judgmental response of others. You will also learn to seek out the support of those who naturally adopt a "companioning" attitude toward you and avoid those who do not.

How To Use This Book

One primary purpose of this book is to provide an opportunity for you to learn about your own unique journey into and through the divorce experience. As you have without doubt already discovered, divorce and the grief that accompanies it are intensely personal experiences. No two people experience divorce in exactly the same way. Your own experience is unlike anyone else's, even though you will probably find that you share some commonalities with other people going through the experience. I hope you discover this book to be a "safe place" to embrace what you uniquely think and feel without fear of being judged.

One of the concerns I have about many books written about divorce is that they try to tell you, the reader, what to think and feel. Worse yet, they may subtly or directly shame you for getting a divorce. Another theme you will discover in many

Companioning Versus Treating

The word "treat" comes from the Latin root "tractare," which means "to drag." On the other hand, the word "companion," when broken down into is original Latin roots, means "messmate" (*com* for "with" and *pan* for "bread"). Someone you would share a meal with, a friend, an equal. I have taken liberties with the noun "companion" and made it into the verb "companioning" because it so well captures the type of helping relationship I support and advocate.

More specifically, for me...

- Companioning is about honoring the spirit; it is not about focusing on the intellect.
- Companioning is about curiosity; it is not about expertise.
- Companioning is about learning from others; it is not about leading.
- Companioning is about being still; it is not about frantic movement forward.
- Companioning is about discovering the gifts of sacred silence; it is not about filling every painful moment with talk.
- Companioning is about listening with the heart; it is not about analyzing with the head.
- Companioning is about bearing witness to the struggles of others; it is not about directing those struggles.
- Companioning is about being present to another person's pain; it is not about taking away the pain.
- Companioning is about respecting disorder and confusion; it is not about imposing order and logic.
- Companioning is about going to the wilderness of the soul with another human being; it is not about thinking you are responsible for finding the way out.

In your journey through divorce grief, seek out the support of those who naturally adopt a "companioning" attitude toward you and avoid those who do not.

books is the minimization of your need to mourn what you have lost, and an attempt to quickly and prematurely move you forward. This book is decidedly different than that. Actually, I hope to help you go backward, or acknowledge the loss of your hoped-for relationship, before I in any way encourage you to go forward.

"We must always say goodbye to previous intimate relationships before in any way we can authentically say hello to new intimate relationships. Our culture has a tendency to get that out of order."

A.D.W.

This book is also different in another important way: It allows and encourages you to explore how you think and feel right now. While it does describe ten essential Touchstones, you will find that each of these Touchstones will be "lived" and experienced in different ways by different people. The key is not to fit your experience to the Touchstones, but to fit the Touchstones to your experience.

I encourage you to interact with this book. The companion journal to this book (*The Transcending Divorce Journal: Exploring the Ten Essential Touchstones*) even gives you a special place to write out your thoughts and feelings. Neither this book nor the journal attempt to prescribe how you should feel, because to integrate divorce into your life demands that you embrace your own unique responses, thoughts, and feelings.

When you read a section that really speaks to you or gives you a new insight, highlight it and come back to it. You might want to create a time to talk about these meaningful sections with a friend, a counselor, or a support group.

I also invite and encourage you to complete the companion journal. Journaling your experience is a powerful method for helping yourself heal and eventually transcend into a new and meaningful future life. When you feel inspired to expand on your thoughts and feelings about your past, your present, or your future, create some dedicated time to express yourself more completely in your journal. Journaling allows you to express your multitude of thoughts and feelings outside of yourself. Use this resource fully. Integrate it into your daily life and into the depths of your soul. To mourn what you have lost and to transcend is such hard work. It mandates your active participation.

The Value of a Support Group Experience

If you're not a journaler, that's okay too. Not everyone feels comfortable expressing themselves through the written word. Talking about what you're reading in this book with someone who cares and understands, meeting with a compassionate counselor, or joining a support group are other effective ways to integrate the Touchstones and mourn your lost relationship.

In Gratitude

I thank you for taking time to read and reflect on the words that make up this book. This book comes from my heart to yours. It comes from my own discovering of the need to mourn my lost dreams and to eventually contemplate new possibilities for living, growing, and loving. Instead of viewing divorce as a reflection of personal failure, I believe there are usually legitimate and understandable reasons that relationships end.

"The quality and quantity of understanding support you get during your divorce experience will have a major influence on your capacity to not only heal, but to eventually transcend. You cannot—nor should you try to—do this alone. Drawing on the experiences and encouragement of friends, counselors, and fellow travelers in the divorce experience is not a weakness, but rather a healthy human need."

A.D.W.

And when relationships end, we need and deserve unconditional support, not shame and judgment. I hope this book provides you some of the unconditional love you need right now in your life journey. All too many people suffer the trauma of ending an intimate relationship alone and in isolation. Yet, we all need "companions" if we are to survive and eventually thrive. Again, I hope this book becomes a reliable companion into and through the ten Touchstones that follow.

And remember that good self-care is essential for you right now. To practice good self-care doesn't mean you are feeling sorry for yourself or are selfish; rather, it means you are being compassionate with yourself and allowing yourself to heal. For it is in nurturing yourself, in allowing yourself the time and loving attention you need to mourn your lost marriage, that you will eventually find meaning in your continued living. It is in having the courage to care for your own needs that you will eventually discover a fullness to live and love again.

If you find this book helpful, write to me about your journey and allow me to learn from you. Again, I thank you from deep in my soul for having the courage to explore the Touchstones I have provided in this resource. I hope we meet one day!

Alan D. Wolfelt, Ph.D.

Center for Loss and Life Transition
Fort Collins, Colorado

Touchstone One

Open to the Presence of Your Loss

"In every heart there is an inner room, where we can hold our greatest treasures and our deepest pain."

Marianne Williamson

You are going through or have experienced a divorce. In your heart, you have come to know deep pain. From my own divorce experience as well as those of thousands of people I have companioned over the years, I have learned that we cannot go around the pain that is the wilderness of our grief surrounding lost love. Instead, we must journey all through it, sometimes shuffling along the less strenuous side paths, sometimes plowing directly into the dark center.

In opening to the presence of the pain of your divorce, in acknowledging the inevitability of the pain, in being willing to gently embrace the pain, you in effect honor the pain. "What?" you naturally protest, "honor the pain?" Crazy as it may sound, your pain is the key that opens your heart and ushers you on your way to eventual healing and transcendence.

You see, it is impossible to accept what you have not faced. You cannot integrate what you have not grasped or felt. The struggles that accompany divorce cannot be avoided. As difficult as it is to do, you must squarely face your pain.

In many ways, and as strange as it may seem, this book is intended to help you honor the pain that comes with your divorce. Even if you are the one who initiated the divorce, pain accompanies the experience. Honoring means recognizing the value of and respecting. It is not instinctive to see grief and the need to openly mourn your divorce as something to honor, yet the end of your marriage brings about a necessity to mourn. Honoring the grief surrounding your divorce is not self-destructive or harmful; it is self-sustaining and life-giving!

> *"If we resist the pain of ending, we skirt the opportunity for initiation."*
> Thomas Moore

You have probably been taught that pain is an indication that something is wrong and that you should find ways to alleviate the pain. In our culture, pain and feelings of loss are experiences most people try to avoid. Why? Because the role of pain and suffering is misunderstood. Normal thoughts and feelings after losses of any kind (divorce, death, etc.) are often seen as unnecessary and inappropriate.

You will probably learn over time that the pain of your divorce grief will keep trying to get your attention until you have the courage to gently, and in small doses, open to its presence. The alternative—denying or suppressing your pain—is in fact more painful.

Denial—not admitting, actively trying to forget, not letting yourself know or recognize a difficult truth about yourself and your divorce experience—is a psychological position that most of us who have walked this walk have needed to use at some point in the journey. Denial protects us from the pain of loss and the need to mourn. But denial is a temporary time-out and ultimately can become far worse than facing the pain that comes with divorce loss. Actually, when you get stuck in denial that your marriage has ended (or is ending), it represents a spiritual compromise, a disability that limits your potential growth and transcendence on every level.

I have learned that the pain that surrounds the closed heart is the pain of living against yourself. You run the risk of withdrawing and experiencing greater isolation and aloneness. A closed heart renders you unable to love and be loved by those who are available and willing to surround you in unconditional love. So, I invite you to choose courage and face any denial surrounding your divorce. For behind your denial hides a beautiful, radiant spirit, a new, whole, conscious self just waiting to face the truth, to finally be born. As we just get started on this journey together, I want to begin by welcoming you to what can and will become a new, hope-filled world. This is the kind of world that awaits you.

What is Healing?

To heal literally means to become whole again. Healing is the process of integrating your grief into your self and learning ways to live your changed life with fullness and meaning. Experiencing a new and changed "wholeness" requires that you engage in the work of mourning. It doesn't just happen to you; you must stay open to that which has broken you for healing to begin.

Healing is a holistic concept that embraces the physical, emotional, cognitive, social and spiritual realms. Note that healing is not the same as *curing*, which is a medical term that means "remedying" or "correcting." You cannot remedy your grief, but you can integrate it into your life. You cannot correct your grief, but you can heal it.

You have a choice. Yes, you can choose to allow yourself to remain open to the pain. As an ancient Hebrew sage observed, "If you want life, you must expect suffering." Paradoxically, it is the gathering of the courage to move toward the pain that ultimately leads to healing your wounded heart. By being willing to engage your feelings and honor the truth in them, you are being true to your authentic self.

In part, this book will encourage you to be present to your multitude of thoughts and feelings, to "be with" them, for they contain the truth you are searching for, the energy you may be lacking, and the eventual unfolding of your healing and transcendence. Oh, and keep in mind, you will need *all* of your thoughts and feelings to lead you there, *not just the feelings you judge as acceptable.* For it is in being honest with yourself that you find your way through the wilderness of your divorce and identify the places in you that need to be healed. Yes, grief and mourning are critical ingredients in the life and unfolding of your soul.

Dosing Your Pain

While this first Touchstone seeks to help you understand the role of pain in your healing and eventual transcendence, I want to make sure you also understand that you cannot embrace the pain of your divorce grief all at once. If you were to feel it all at once, you might feel overwhelmed and unsure that you could survive. Instead, you must allow yourself to "dose" the pain—feel it in small waves then allow it to retreat until you are ready for the next wave.

EXPRESS YOURSELF: Go to *The Transcending Divorce Journal*, p. 7.

As you stay present to your pain that comes with the experience of divorce, you will be participating in "soul work," which will eventually lead to "spirit work." Keep in mind that "soul work" precedes "spirit work."

Soul Work: A downward movement in the psyche; a willingness to connect with what is dark, deep and not necessarily pleasant

"A wound that goes unacknowledged and unwept is a wound that cannot heal."

John Eldredge

Spirit Work: A quality of moving toward the light; upward, ascending

In part, healing and transcendence are about your willingness to descend into your soul work on the path to your spirit work. My personal and professional experience suggests that when

we encounter divorce loss, we must descend before we can
transcend.

EXPRESS YOURSELF: Go to *The Transcending Divorce
Journal*, p. 7.

Setting Your Intention to Heal and Transcend

You are on a journey that is naturally frightening, painful and
often lonely. No words, written or spoken, can take away the
pain you feel now. I hope, however, that this book will bring
comfort and encouragement as you make a commitment to
embracing that very pain.

It takes a true commitment to heal your divorce grief. Yes, you
are wounded, but with commitment and intention you can and
will become whole again. Commitment goes hand in hand with
the concept of "setting your intention." Intention is defined as
being conscious of what you want to experience. A close cousin
of "affirmation," it is using the power of positive thought to
produce a desired result. So, how can you use this concept of
setting your intention to influence your journey through the grief
that comes with lost love?

When you set your intention to heal and eventually transcend
this life-changing experience, you make a true commitment
to positively influence the course of your journey. You choose
between being what I call a "passive witness" or an "active
participant" in your divorce experience. I'm sure you have heard
this tired cliché: Time heals all wounds. Yet, time alone has
nothing to do with healing the wounds of grief that come with
divorce. Healing and integrating this loss into your life demands
that you engage actively in the grief journey. It can't be fixed or
resolved; it can only be soothed and integrated through actively
experiencing the multitude of thoughts and feelings involved.

Integrating Your Divorce Grief

The concept of intention-setting presupposes that your outer
reality is a direct reflection of your inner thoughts and beliefs. If

you can change or mold some of your thoughts and beliefs, then you can influence your reality. In journaling and speaking (and praying!) your intentions, you actively help "set" them.

You might tell yourself, "I can and will reach out for support during this difficult time in my life. I will become filled with hope that I can and will survive this divorce." Together with these words, you might form mental pictures of hugging and talking to your friends and seeing happier times in your future.

Integration

An important concept to keep in mind as you journey through the grief of your divorce experience is that of integration. You cannot "get over" or "resolve" your grief from divorce loss, but you can learn to integrate it. That is, you can learn to incorporate it into your consciousness and proceed with meaning and purpose in your life. See Touchstone Nine for more on the concept of integration.

Setting your intention to heal is not only a way of surviving your divorce (although it is indeed that!), it is a way of actively guiding your grief. Of course, you will still have to honor and embrace your pain during this time. By honoring the presence of your pain, by understanding the appropriateness of your pain, you are committing to facing the pain. You are committing yourself to pay attention to your experience in ways that allow you to eventually begin to breathe life into your soul again. What better reason to give attention to your intention! The alternative would be to shut down in an effort to avoid and deny your pain (see my book *Living in the Shadow of the Ghosts of Grief*), which is to die inside while you are still alive.

In reality, denying your grief, running from it, or minimizing it only seems to make it more confusing and overwhelming. Paradoxically, to eventually soften your hurt, you must embrace it. As strange as it may seem, you must make it your friend.

In this book, I will attempt to teach you to gently and lovingly befriend your divorce grief. To not be so afraid to express your grief. To not be ashamed of your tears and profound feelings of sadness. To try not to pull down the blinds that shut out light and love. Slowly, and in "doses," you can and will return to life and begin to live in ways that put stars back into your sky.

EXPRESS YOURSELF: Go to *The Transcending Divorce Journal*, p. 9.

No Reward for Speed

Reconciling your divorce grief does not happen quickly or efficiently. The "grief work" surrounding divorce may be some of the hardest work you ever do. Because grief is work, it calls on your physical, emotional, cognitive, social, and spiritual energy.

Consequently, you must be patient with yourself. When you come to trust that the pain will not last forever, it becomes tolerable. Deceiving yourself into thinking that the pain does not even exist is sure to make

Spiritual Pessimism Versus Spiritual Optimism

In part, you can choose whether you intend to experience spiritual pessimism or spiritual optimism. For example, if you believe getting a divorce means you are an inferior person who has a multitude of character flaws, it will be next to impossible for you to make it through this difficult time. By contrast, if you "set your intention" to recognize that embracing the pain of your loss can help you to integrate this experience, you can and will survive. In addition, if you can acknowledge life's mysterious forces, then without overlooking the pain, you might actually see some wisdom in the relationship ending. So, ask yourself, will you be a spiritual pessimist surrounding your divorce, or will you be a spiritual optimist?

it intolerable. Spiritual maturity in your grief work is attained when you embrace a paradox: to live at once in the state of both encounter and surrender, to both "work at" and "surrender to" your grief.

As you come to know this paradox, you will slowly discover the soothing of your soul. Resist the need to figure out everything with your head, and let the paradox embrace you. You will find yourself wrapped in a gentle peace—the peace of living at once in both *encounter* (feeling the pain of your grief) and *surrender*

Understanding the Concept of Surrender

This concept of surrender teaches you that when you stop resisting and surrender to your situation exactly as it is, things begin to change. Resistance is an instinctive defense mechanism you use to push away or deny your pain, to protect you from your feelings of loss and grief. In the end, resistance robs you of your capacity to heal and transcend. When you surrender, you acknowledge, "This is what I am faced with right now in my life's journey. While I'd like it to be different, I must allow myself to face the reality of what is happening." When you surrender, you release attachment to how you feel your life should be and invite yourself to be in the presence of your life exactly as it is. Surrender is an act of courage that allows you to detach from the outcome. In surrender, you become more capable of living in the reality of the here and now—more capable of seeing choices that were concealed from you. In surrender, you may also find consolation that, in some strange, mysterious way beyond your control, the relationship you had with the person you were married to has been fulfilled. In surrender, you are invited to stop trying to control what you cannot control. The gifts of peace of mind and gentleness of heart awaits you.

(embracing the mystery without trying to "understand" it with your head).

EXPRESS YOURSELF: Go to *The Transcending Divorce Journal*, p. 9.

Face Any Inappropriate Expectations

You are at risk for having inappropriate expectations of how "well" you should be doing in the face of your divorce experience. These expectations result from common societal messages that tell you to "be strong" in the face of life losses. Invariably, some people around you will say things like: "You just need to move on." "You are better off without him (or her)." "He (or she) wasn't right for you anyway." "Keep your chin up." "Keep busy." And my personal favorite, which I heard numerous times: "I've got someone for you to meet."

"It does not matter how slowly you go, so long as you do not stop."

Confucius

Often combined with these messages is an unstated but strong belief that "You have a right not to hurt. So do whatever is necessary to avoid it." The unfortunate result is that you may be encouraged by some people around you to be happy when you need to be sad, self-treat your pain with drugs or alcohol, prematurely involve yourself in a new relationship, or deny any and all feelings of loss and grief.

Society often tends to make those of us who experience divorce loss feel ashamed and embarrassed about our pain and grief. Shame can be described as the feeling that something you are doing is bad or wrong. And you may feel that if you mourn the loss of your marriage, then you should be ashamed. If you internalize these messages, you

"To suppress the grief, the pain, is to condemn oneself to a living death. Living fully means feeling fully; it means being completely one with what you are experiencing and not holding it at arm's length."

Phillip Kapleau

will, in fact, feel like a failure. Sad to say, if you are perceived as "doing well" with your divorce by social standards, you are considered "strong," "holding up very well," and "in control." By contrast, if your feelings are fairly intense, you may be labeled "overly-emotional" or "needy." I often observe that society has it backwards about who is "doing well" in times of grief and loss and who is "not doing well." Naturally, if you avoid the pain that accompanies the loss of your marriage, the people around you will not have to "be with" you in your pain or experience any pain that might be influencing their own lives. While this may be more comfortable for them, it would prove to be unhealthy for you. The reality is that many people will try to shield themselves from pain by trying to protect you from yours. Do not let anyone do this to you!

When your personal feelings of grief are met with shame-based messages, discovering how to heal yourself becomes more difficult. If you internalize these messages that encourage repression of grief, you may even become tempted to act as if you feel better than you really do. Ultimately, however, if you deny the emotions of your heart, you deny the essence of your life.

EXPRESS YOURSELF: Go to *The Transcending Divorce Journal*, p. 10.

Staying Open to the Ripple Effects of Divorce

When you experience divorce, there is a huge ripple effect of additional loss that spreads out in many directions. Let's inventory these potential additional losses. You may even want to place a checkmark beside those that apply to you. Obviously this list is not all-inclusive, and I encourage you to add other specific losses to this list that apply to your unique experience.

- *Loss of dreams and goals.* Many aspects of hopes and dreams you had together as a couple are now changed and different.

- *Loss of self-esteem.* When you experience divorce loss, it is natural that your self-esteem is impacted. You may not feel as attractive and desirable as you once did.

- *Loss of identity, belonging and lifestyle.* The whole is always greater than the sum of its parts. You were part of a "couple" and a "family." Divorce can leave you feeling uncertain of your identity and leave you questioning where you "belong" in the world around you. Your lifestyle is different than when you were part of a "couple."

- *Loss of personality.* In part, you knew who you were because you had a "mirror" in your life. When you lose your mirror, you may find yourself reflecting, "I just don't feel like myself."

- *Loss of feeling loved and accepted.* Love is anchored in acceptance. The loss of love can put you at risk for feeling unacceptable, unlovable or unworthy of love. This may also impact your ability to trust others.

- *Loss of someone to express love to.* Giving love is as important as receiving love. You may feel like you have love to give, but no one is there to receive it.

- *Loss of intimacy needs.* You may miss someone holding you, touching you, making love with you. While this is difficult for many to acknowledge, loss of emotional, physical and sexual intimacy are tremendous losses for many divorced people.

- *Loss of companionship and a partnership.* You may have been used to doing things together that you now need to do alone. It may have been little things like watching TV together, going shopping together, just being in the same room together. Now even these "little" things feel very different and result in feelings of sadness and aloneness.

- *Loss of physical security.* You may not feel as safe living alone as you did when you lived with your spouse. A very wise person once noted, "I didn't know that grief felt so much like fear."

- *Loss of financial security.* You may have gone from two incomes to one income, yet have increased expenses with all the changes that come with the divorce. You may have to learn to manage finances in ways you didn't before.

- *Loss of your home.* Dorothy was so right: "There's no place like home." You may miss your kitchen or your garden. Now

25

you may live somewhere else and it feels very different. You may have had to downsize and miss the space you used to enjoy.

- *Loss of good credit.* Your ability to be approved for loans may be impacted. You may feel like you are rebuilding your financial life, and this can leave you feeling a loss of power at a time when you may already feel helpless.

- *Loss of friends and family.* Your friendships and family relationships are no doubt impacted by the divorce. You may have been close to some of your spouse's family, but those relationships have now been cut off. Some friends can't seem to be supportive of you and may stay away. Sometimes family and friends are judgmental and stop all communication or, sadly, even harass you for the decisions you have made.

- *Loss of reputation.* Does anyone whisper when you pass? Does anyone spread rumors about you or your former spouse? Sometimes with divorce there are aspects of loss of reputation that may hurt deeply.

- *Loss of faith.* You may be questioning your faith or spirituality. This can result in a lost sense of meaning and purpose in your life. Some people may judge you or reject you from faith perspectives, which may leave you feeling alone and rejected.

- *Loss of joy and happiness.* Some of life's most precious emotions, such as joy and happiness, can be compromised by the experience of divorce.

- *Loss of health.* Divorce can compromise your immune system and result in changes in your health. Difficulty with sleeping and changes in eating patterns are very common. Other health changes might include headaches, muscle aches, lethargy, irritable bowel, skin reactions, difficulty with concentration and confusion. Obviously, our bodies are tied into our emotions and let us know when we are stressed out.

- *Loss of your children.* You may have lost custody or have to share custody of your children. Moving children back and forth between homes is a loss in and of itself. Not seeing your children every day or being able to put them to bed at night is a very real loss.

- *Loss of influence over your children.* If you are not with your children as much as you were before, you can experience a loss of influence over what they see, hear and do. You may experience a parental instinct to protect them but feel helpless to do so.

- *Loss of your children's loyalty.* The reality is that sometimes children take sides around who is "right" and who is "wrong" in a divorce. Sometimes children are encouraged to choose a "side," and you feel cut off from them.

- *Loss of the hope for future children.* Perhaps you had hopes to have more children in the future. The loss that comes with divorce can also bring real loss related to future children.

- *Loss of hope for a future marriage or significant relationship.* Some divorced people feel hopeless about the possibility of meeting and committing to another mate. You may feel like you had your chance and now doubt a meaningful relationship will come your way again.

EXPRESS YOURSELF: Go to *The Transcending Divorce Journal*, p. 11.

Divorce Grief is Not a Disease

Obviously, you have discovered that this resource is intended to help you openly acknowledge and mourn the losses that come with your divorce experience. You have also probably already realized that no quick fix exists for the pain you are enduring. But I promise that if you can think, feel and see yourself as an active participant in your healing, you will experience a renewed sense of meaning and purpose in your life. Yes,

> *"We have to do the best we can. This is our sacred human responsibility."*
>
> Albert Einstein

this book is different than most books on divorce. It is about mourning well before going forward with your life. Why? Because I firmly believe that it is through mourning our divorce loss and all that comes with it that we eventually transcend and are able to experience new life.

Please allow me to remind you that divorce grief is not a disease. To be human means to experience and know loss as part of your life. Many losses or "little griefs" occur along life's path. You may find that not all of your losses are as painful as others; they do not always disconnect you from yourself. But your divorce from a person you once gave love to and received love from is likely to leave you feeling disconnected from both yourself and the outside world.

While the grief that accompanies divorce is a powerful experience, so, too, is your ability to help facilitate your own healing. In this moment, you are demonstrating your commitment and setting your intentions to reinvest in life and living. How? Through your willingness to read and reflect on the pages in this book, complete the companion journal (at your own pace) and participate in some form of a support group with other fellow travelers.

I invite you to gently confront the pain of your grief. I will try with all of my heart to point to the Touchstones as you journey through the wilderness of your divorce grief. As we go forward, remember: As you do your grief work you will experience transcendence and live with meaning and purpose every day of your life.

"We might find that an ending is a door opening into an unknown and promising world."

Thomas Moore

EXPRESS YOURSELF: Go to *The Transcending Divorce Journal*, p. 11.

Touchstone Two

Dispel the Misconceptions About Divorce and Grief

Misconception

A misconception is a mistaken notion you might have about something—in other words, something you believe to be true but isn't. Misconceptions about divorce are common in our society. You can see how we'd have misconceptions about something as emotional as divorce.

As you journey through the wilderness of your divorce grief, if you mourn openly and authentically, you will come to find a path that feels right for you. This path will be your path to healing and eventual transcendence. But beware—others may try to pull you off this path. They may try to make you believe that the path you have chosen is wrong, even "crazy," and that their way is better.

The reason that people try to pull you off the path to healing and transcendence is that they have internalized some common misconceptions about the divorce experience. Many of the misconceptions, in essence, deny you your right to hurt and authentically mourn your lost hopes and dreams for your marriage. They often can lead us to have unrealistic expectations about the divorce experience.

As you read about this important Touchstone, you may discover that you yourself have believed in some of these misconceptions and that some of the people close to you may embrace them as well. Don't condemn yourself or others for believing these misconceptions. Instead, make use of any new insights you might gain as you explore these because this will help open your heart to your work of mourning in ways that will restore your soul.

"Learning about these misconceptions has helped me so much. The new insights I experienced made such a difference in how I feel about myself and my divorce."

Mary Francis

You will see that at the end of the discussion of each misconception I have included an affirmation to help you declare your intent to transcend the misconceptions about divorce and grief. I hope you will use these affirmations to help you find your way in this part of your divorce journey.

Misconception 1
Grief and mourning are the same thing.

Perhaps you have noticed that people tend to use the words "grieving" and "mourning" interchangeably. There is an important distinction, however. We as humans move toward integrating loss (divorce loss included) into our lives not just by grieving, but by mourning. You will move toward transcendence not just by grieving, but through active and intentional mourning of your lost relationship.

Grief is the constellation of internal thoughts and feelings we have when we experience divorce. Think of grief as the container. It holds all of your thoughts, feelings, and images of your experience when you go through a divorce. In other words, grief is the internal meaning you give to your divorce experience.

Mourning, in contrast, is when you take the grief you have inside and express it outside of yourself. Another way of defining mourning is "grief gone public" or the "outward expression of grief."

Especially in a society that tends to "hurry people up" surrounding issues of loss and grief, you must remember to allow yourself time to fully grieve and mourn. Until you integrate your thoughts and feelings about your marriage and divorce, these thoughts and feelings will keep trying to get you to give them the attention they deserve. It is through active mourning of what you have lost that you eventually discover new life.

> *"We may need to acknowledge that this experience of grief and mourning is an essential part of the soul's life."*
>
> Thomas Moore

Obviously, this book is rooted in the importance of openly and honestly mourning the loss of your relationship by expressing your grief outside of yourself. Over time and with the support of others, mourning will create momentum for your healing.

WARNING: When you divorce, some well-meaning but misinformed friends and family may encourage you to "keep it to yourself" and "move on with your life quickly." If you take these kinds of messages to heart, the disastrous result will be that all of your thoughts and feelings will stay neatly bottled up inside you.

So, from my heart to yours, I gently remind you that a catalyst for eventual transcendence can only be created when you have the courage to mourn in the presence of understanding, compassionate people who will not judge you. I should mention that the compassionate companions are often people who have walked through a divorce of their own. For this very reason, a support group may be of great help. At times, of course, you will grieve alone, but expressing your grief outside of yourself in the presence of others is necessary.

When you don't give attention to your divorce experience by acknowledging it first to yourself and then to those around you, the grief will accumulate. Then the denied, inhibited grief will likely come flowing out of you in all sorts of negative ways (e.g., chronic depression, anxiety disorders, physical complaints, addictive behaviors), compounding the pain of your divorce.

Expressing Feelings and Creating Perturbation

Our feelings are the way we perceive ourselves. They allow us to respond to the world around us and help us know that we are alive. That is why when you shut them down, you risk being among the "living dead." When we lose touch with our feelings, we have no true awareness of life.

Actually, the word "feeling" comes from the Indo-European root that means "touch." To feel is to activate your capacity to be touched and changed by experiences that you encounter along life's path—in this situation, your divorce. This is what creates the movement and flow in your life. The term "perturbation" refers to the capacity to experience change and movement. The purpose of mourning is to allow feelings to move through you in ways that integrate them into your life.

To integrate grief into your life requires that you are "touched" by what you experience. When you cannot feel a feeling, you are closed in your ability to use it or be changed by it, and instead of experiencing perturbation, you become "stuck." This can result in being out of touch with your feelings and will lead you down a path to carrying the grief surrounding your divorce. (For more information and insight on carried grief, see my book *Living in the Shadow of the Ghosts of Grief.*)

When you carry your grief, not only do you struggle to identify what you are feeling, you often have difficulty expressing feelings to people around you. Your capacity to experience life fully is inhibited, and you begin to shut down. In contrast, you can see that other people are "touched" by what happens to them and to others. They recognize they have special needs when losses impact their lives. They feel deeply and show it. They are not stoic in the face of loss but respond to the instinct to organically mourn openly and honestly.

The word "emotion" literally means "energy in motion." To be authentic surrounding your emotions is to have them work for you instead of against you. To do that requires that you put your emotion into motion through mourning.

So, do not just grieve your lost marriage, mourn your lost marriage. As you do your mourning work, you will begin to experience the rewards of being in touch with your authentic feelings and the resulting perturbation. Then you will experience the benefits of authentic mourning and start to glimpse enhanced feelings of aliveness, curiosity and spontaneity.

DECLARE YOUR INTENT:

Place your hand on your heart and say out loud…

"*Mourning allows feelings to move through me in ways that integrate them into my life.*"

Put your hand on your head and say out loud…

"*I will survive and transcend this divorce.*"

EXPRESS YOURSELF: Go to *The Transcending Divorce Journal*, p. 14.

Misconception 2
If you get a divorce, you are a failure.

There are those people out there who may project to you that when your marriage ends, you are a failure as a person. Nothing could be further from the truth.

Divorce is about the disintegration of hopes and dreams, about a life partner who did not materialize. Integrating this loss into your life is naturally painful and challenging, but I urge you to remember that you are not a failure.

Remind yourself frequently that divorce is not failure, it is a transition. Because a marriage doesn't last an entire lifetime does not mean that you have failed or that you are a failure. We are conditioned by society to bring to marriage many unrealistic expectations, such as "two shall become one," "until death do us part," and, of course, "happily every after." Actually, in a healthy partnership, two people remain separate individuals who communicate respect for each other, perceive each other as equals, and grow both individually and together. The reality is that for many, it takes more than one try to both discover and experience this kind of equal and mutually satisfying relationship.

"For some reason, we see divorce as a signal of failure, despite the fact that each of us has a right, and an obligation, to rectify any other mistake we make in life."

Dr. Joyce Brothers

To give some perspective, allow me to remind you that close to half of all marriages end in divorce. You are not a failure. You are not odd or unusual. And you are not alone. In contemporary times, where we are fortunate to live much longer than previous generations, we change many aspects of our lives with greater frequency. Change is an option that prior generations did not have. As we become more aware of the human lifecycle across time, it is obvious that many stable people with strong values do change as different stages of life and living evolve. Sometimes these changes will include the need to have a marriage come to an end. I urge you to view this new phase of life as a quest. It is an opportunity to mature, cultivate new interests, learn new skills, make mistakes and learn from them. No, you are not a failure. You are a human being who has found herself or himself mourning the loss of a dream. Allow yourself to mourn but do not masochistically punish yourself out of some sense of failure.

DECLARE YOUR INTENT:

Place your hand on your heart and say out loud…

"I am not a failure."

Put your hand on your head and say out loud…

"I will survive and transcend this divorce."

EXPRESS YOURSELF: Go to *The Transcending Divorce Journal*, p. 16.

Misconception 3
When you marry, you must stay committed to the thought that this love will last forever.

Many people go into marriage with the thought and hope that marriage is forever. Yes, many people grow up believing that one ideal person completes them and that after they find one another, they will live happily ever after.

Yet, in reality, relationships do end. No, we don't always understand why they end, but they do. Again, approximately one of every two marriages ends in divorce. This fact

> *"If marriage means you fell in love, does divorce mean you climbed out?"*
>
> Anonymous

demonstrates that love is often not forever. This misconception related to "forever" often results in us judging ourselves harshly when our relationships end. As a consequence, you are at risk for feeling guilty that the relationship did not last a lifetime.

Relationships sometimes have a lifetime of their own that does not always include forever. So, yours did not last forever, and you are faced with the need to mourn your lost dreams, your lost love. But this doesn't mean you are some kind of terrible person. A relationship is not always the final resting place where you settle in forever. Again, mourn your loss, but do not self-punish in ways that play into this misconception.

DECLARE YOUR INTENT:

Place your hand on your heart and say out loud…

"Not all marriages are intended to last forever."

Put your hand on your head and say out loud…

"I will survive and transcend this divorce."

EXPRESS YOURSELF: Go to *The Transcending Divorce Journal*, p. 17.

Misconception 4
Divorce is a modern affliction.

Some people would have you believe that divorces have only been taking place in the recent past. Actually, divorces have been with us since marriages have been with us. You may hear people provide doom-and-gloom criticisms of contemporary society and how it is only in the very recent past that divorce came into existence. However, history demonstrates otherwise.

Divorce has been with us at least since the earliest written records. The ancient Athenians divorced, as did citizens of the Roman Empire. The practice of annulment was also common throughout history. The first divorce in the United States actually took place in the early 1600s! Divorce has been with us for many, many years and it will continue to be with us. Again, you are not alone or the only one to walk through this wilderness.

DECLARE YOUR INTENT:

Place your hand on your heart and say out loud...

"Divorce has been part of society for a very long time. I am not alone in going through this experience."

Put your hand on your head and say out loud...

"I will survive and transcend this divorce."

EXPRESS YOURSELF: Go to *The Transcending Divorce Journal*, p. 18.

Misconception 5
If you get a divorce, you will never marry again.

Some people would have you believe that if you get a divorce, you will never have another significant relationship or ever marry again. However, I remind you that divorce is not necessarily a permanent state. It is often a transition to single-hood, re-coupling, or eventual remarriage.

The reality is that many people do eventually remarry. Actually, about three out of four North Americans who get divorced remarry, usually within three

"The first step to a healthy remarriage is you."

Jeff and Judi Parziale

years. Yet, naturally many people have the fear that if they divorce they will never love or be loved ever again. The truth is that divorce does not make you unloveable or unloving, as this misconception would have you believe.

I have companioned many people through the divorce process: people who didn't want the relationship to end; people who initiated the end of the relationship; and people who mutually agreed with each other to end the relationship. My experience has been that regardless of the specifics related to the "ending," if you are willing to authentically mourn your loss, you can go on to create new and satisfying intimate partnerships.

DECLARE YOUR INTENT:

Place your hand on your heart and say out loud…

"Should I so choose, I am very capable of eventually going forward to establish a new intimate partnership."

Put your hand on your head and say out loud…

"I will survive and transcend this divorce."

EXPRESS YOURSELF: Go to *The Transcending Divorce Journal*, p. 19.

Misconception 6
The grief and mourning of divorce loss progress in predictable, orderly stages.

Probably you have heard about the "stages" of grief that follow a straight, linear path.

This type of thinking about the experience of divorce is appealing, but inaccurate. Many people like to believe that the path through divorce is a direct path. Yet nothing could be further from the truth. Instead of being predictable and orderly, it is more often complex and unpredictable. Rather than being smooth, it often has plenty of bumps as well as twists and turns. Sometimes you might even encounter a pothole or two!

The concept of "stages" related to the grief experience was popularized in 1969 with the publication of Elisabeth Kübler-Ross' landmark book *On Death and Dying*. In this important book, Dr. Kübler-Ross described five stages of grief she observed when people were dying: denial, anger, bargaining, depression, and acceptance. However, Dr. Kübler-Ross never intended for her stages to be interpreted as a rigid, linear sequence to be followed by anyone and everyone who has a loss in their lives. Some people have made direct application of those "stages" to divorce loss, which has resulted in self-doubt and confusion for many divorced people.

> *"To spare oneself from grief at all costs can be achieved only at the price of total detachment, which excludes the ability to experience happiness."*
>
> Erich Fromm

WARNING: You may have some well-meaning, misinformed people around you project a rigid system of beliefs about the "stages" of grief related to your divorce. And if you have internalized this misconception, you may also find yourself trying to prescribe "stages" to your own divorce experience. Instead of allowing yourself to be where you are, you may try to force yourself to be in another "stage" or be upset because you are not where you are "supposed to be" in terms of these stages.

For example, the common responses of confusion and disorganization, anxiety and fear, guilt, sadness, and/or protest emotions may or may not occur during your unique divorce experience. Or feelings of relief may occur and overlap with another part of your response. Sometimes your emotions may follow each other in a short period of time. At other times, two or more emotions may be present simultaneously. Remember—do not try to determine where you "should" be. Just allow yourself to be naturally where you are as the process unfolds.

Everyone encounters divorce in different ways. Don't think your goal is to move through prescribed stages of grief. As you read further in this book, you will find that a major theme is to help you become aware that your grief is unique. The word "unique" literally means "only one." No one ever existed exactly like you before, and no one will be exactly like you again. As part of the divine healing process, the thoughts and feelings you will experience will be totally unique to you.

DECLARE YOUR INTENT:

Place your hand on your heart and say out loud...

"There are no linear, predictable or orderly 'stages' to my divorce experience. I will probably experience some twists and turns along the way."

Put your hand on your head and say out loud...

"I will survive and transcend this divorce."

EXPRESS YOURSELF: Go to *The Transcending Divorce Journal*, p. 19.

Misconception 7
You should try not to think or feel about the person you are divorcing (or have divorced) on holidays, anniversaries, and birthdays.

As with all things involving grief, loss and major change, trying not to think and feel about something that your heart and soul are encouraging you to think and feel about is a bad idea. On special occasions, such as holidays, anniversaries (of wedding dates, the day your divorce was finalized, etc.) and birthdays (your birthday or the birthday of the person you are divorced from), it's natural for your grief to well up inside you and spill over, even long after the divorce is over.

It may seem logical to avoid thinking about your ex on these special days. After all, if you can keep very busy, with no time for thinking and feeling, maybe you can avoid some heartache. What I would ask you is this: Where does the heartache go if you don't let it out when it naturally arises? It doesn't disappear. It simply bides its time, patiently at first, then urgently, like a caged animal pacing behind the bars.

If you feel sad or vulnerable during these times, remember: The feelings are honest expressions of the real you. Be gentle to yourself during these times. To respond this way does not mean you are "feeling sorry for yourself;" it means you have "special needs" that must be given attention. As you give attention to your needs, these thoughts and feelings will soften over time.

Some of your friends and family may attempt to perpetuate this misconception. Some people will believe that if they can keep you busy, they can prevent you from feeling your feelings connected to the divorce. While these people are well-intentioned, you will be better served being around people who encourage you to openly express whatever you are thinking and feeling. I remind you that denying feelings does not make them go away. Instead, befriending feelings will help soften them.

DECLARE YOUR INTENT:

Place your hand on your heart and say out loud…

"It is normal and natural for me to think about and have feelings about the person I have divorced on holidays, anniversaries and birthdays."

Put your hand on your head and say out loud…

"I will survive and transcend this divorce."

EXPRESS YOURSELF: Go to *The Transcending Divorce Journal*, p. 20.

Misconception 8
After you get a divorce, the goal should be to "get over it" and "move on" as quickly as possible.

You may have already had people say things to you like, "Are you over it yet?" "Have you moved on?" Or, even worse, maybe you've been told, "Well, you should be over it by now!"

Our culture tends to be impatient with experiences that involve grief, loss and the need to mourn. Don't be shocked when some people around you expect you to be "back to normal" very soon after your divorce.

If you openly express grief outwardly, you may be viewed by some as "weak," "crazy" or "self-pitying." The sometime subtle but direct message is "shape up and get on with your life." This reality is tragic. Some people around you may view your divorce as something to be overcome rather than felt and experienced.

If you internalize these kinds of messages, you may be tempted to repress (bottle up) your thoughts and feelings about the divorce. By doing so, you may be at risk for refusing to befriend your emotions. Disallowing tears, suffering in silence, and "being strong" are often considered admirable behaviors in our culture. Many people have internalized society's message that any mourning surrounding the grief that accompanies divorce should be done quietly, quickly and efficiently. Don't let this message interfere with your natural need to mourn this transition.

"Life is like an onion. You peel it off one layer at a time, and sometimes you weep."

Carl Sandburg

After a divorce, many of us are naturally asked the question, "How are you doing?" We may find ourselves instinctively answering with the clichéd response, "I'm fine." In doing so, you are trying to say to those around you, "I'm not mourning; I have moved on." Of course, friends, family and coworkers may encourage this stance. Why? Because they don't want to talk about the divorce, and they would like to think you are "over it."

If you project to the world around you that you are "fine" and "over it," it seems to be more socially acceptable.

This collaborative pretense about mourning the end of your marriage, however, does not meet your needs in grief. When your grief is ignored, minimized or denied, you will probably feel more alone and isolated in your journey. Ultimately, you may well experience some aspects of the "going crazy" syndrome. (See Touchstone Five.) Masking or moving away from how you actually feel about your major life change creates anxiety, confusion and depression. If you receive little or no social recognition of what this experience is really like for you, you may begin to fear that your thoughts and feelings are abnormal.

Remember—society will often encourage you to prematurely move away from and "get over" your divorce loss. You must continually remind yourself that leaning toward, not away from, the pain that accompanies this major life transition will actually make your eventual healing easier.

To think that as a human being you "get over" your divorce is ludicrous! Rather, if you do the work, you will integrate it into your life. You will be changed in some ways forever by this experience. Then, eventually, you will go on to live a life that allows you to authentically experience the world in new ways, as your transformed self. Yes, you learn to accommodate the divorce and the many losses that accompany it into the fabric of your being.

We will explore more about this important distinction between "getting over" and "living with" in Touchstone Nine. For now, suffice it to say that we do not "get over" our divorce experiences, we are changed by them. Unfortunately, when the people around you think you have to "get over" or "let go of" your grief, they actually encourage you to become a carrier of grief.

DECLARE YOUR INTENT:

Place your hand on your heart and say out loud...

"Integrating this divorce experience into my life is not about 'getting over it' and 'moving on,' or 'letting go.' It is about integrating it into my life, learning from it, and recognizing how I have been changed by it."

Put our hand on your head and say out loud...

"I will survive and transcend this divorce."

EXPRESS YOURSELF: Go to *The Transcending Divorce Journal*, p. 22.

Misconception 9
Nobody can help you with your divorce transition.

We have all heard people say, "Nobody can help you but yourself," or "Do it on your own." Yet, in reality, perhaps the most compassionate thing you can do for yourself at this difficult time is to selectively reach out for help from others.

Being among a safe group of nonjudgmental, caring friends can help you feel nourished and remind you that there are people around to support and comfort you. These connections will hold you, guide you, and remind you that you are loved. Why encounter this wilderness experience alone when you can have companionship? Transformation and healing come to you when you have the humility and courage to seek the support of people around you.

"The friend who can be silent with us in a moment of despair or confusion, who can stay with us in an hour of grief and bereavement, who can tolerate not knowing, not curing, not healing and face with us the reality of our powerlessness, that is a friend who cares."

Henri Nouwen

Think of it this way: Grieving and mourning your marriage may be some of the hardest work you ever do. And hard work is less burdensome when others lend a hand. Facing life's greatest challenges is often much easier when there is a team effort. So it should be for you right now. Please do not try to go through this difficult time in your life alone!

Getting support from other people won't take away the pain that accompanies divorce, but it will, over time, make it more bearable. By definition, the mourning of life losses and transitions requires that you get support from sources outside of yourself (after all, mourning is the outward expression of grief). Many people who begin their post-divorce experiences alone and isolated are transformed by becoming part of a larger group of companions. And besides, reaching out for help connects you to people in ways that strengthen the bonds of love and make life seem worth living again. And, I ask you—what could be better than that?

DECLARE YOUR INTENT:

Place your hand on your heart and say out loud…

"I do not have to go through this experience by myself. I can and will reach out to others who can provide me with support and unconditional love."

Put your hand on your head and say out loud…

"I will survive and transcend this divorce."

EXPRESS YOURSELF: Go to *The Transcending Divorce Journal*, p. 25.

Misconception 10
When the grief and mourning of your divorce are integrated into your life, the painful thoughts and feelings will never come up again.

Oh if only this were so. Divorce is a process, not an event. As your experiences have probably already taught you, grief comes in and out like waves from the ocean. Sometimes when you least expect it, a huge wave comes along and pulls your feet right out from under you.

You may have your divorce decree, but that does not mean these waves stop rolling in. Sometimes heightened periods of sadness may leave you feeling overwhelmed. These times seem to come from nowhere and can be frightening and painful. Something

as simple as a sound, a smell
or a phrase can bring on what
I call a "griefburst." Maybe
you hear a special song or visit
a place that once held great
meaning for you and your partner. Yes, there will likely be times
that are characterized by periods of setbacks and breakthroughs,
discouragement and hope, deep sadness and glimpses of genuine
happiness.

*"Winter is come and gone,
But grief returns with
the revolving year."*

Percy Bysshe Shelley

Allow yourself to experience griefbursts without shame or
self-judgment, no matter where or when they occur. Sooner or
later, one will probably happen when you are surrounded by
other people, maybe even strangers. If you would feel more
comfortable, retreat to somewhere more private, or go see
someone you know will understand, when these strong feelings
surface. (For more on griefbursts, see p. 27.)

You will always, for the rest of your life, feel some aspects of
grief and loss over the ending of your relationship. However,
these feelings will one day no longer dominate your daily
existence or be the center of your life. Yet, they will always be
there, in the background, reminding you of the person and the
relationship you were once connected to.

DECLARE YOUR INTENT:

Place your hand on your heart and say out loud...

*"I realize there will be times when I may experience waves
of grief related to my divorce. I can and will survive these
griefbursts."*

Put your hand on your head and say out loud...

"I will survive and transcend this divorce."

EXPRESS YOURSELF: Go to *The Transcending Divorce
Journal*, p. 27.

Keep in mind that the misconceptions about divorce and grief explored in this chapter are certainly not all the misconceptions surrounding divorce. Use the space in *The Transcending Divorce Journal* (p. 28) to note any other misconceptions you feel you have encountered during your divorce experience.

If you find yourself around people who believe in the misconceptions outlined in this chapter, you may experience a heightened sense of isolation and feel very alone. If the people you are closest to you are unable to support you without judging you, seek out others who can offer nonjudgmental love and support.

Usually, the capacity to be supportive without judging is most developed in people who have been on some kind of grief journey themselves and are willing to be empathetically present to you during this difficult time. When you are surrounded by people who can distinguish the misconceptions from the realities surrounding divorce, you can and will experience the healing you deserve.

Touchstone Three

Understand the Uniqueness of Your Divorce Experience

"Whether a marriage fractures with one quick snap or dies a slow death, a powerful bond is broken."
David B. Hawkins

The wilderness of your divorce experience is *your* wilderness. It is a creation of your unique self, the unique person you were married to, and the unique circumstances of your divorce. Your wilderness may be rockier or it could feel more level than that of other people who have experienced divorce. The path to the end of your marriage may have been revealed in a straight line, or it may have been full of twists and turns. In the wilderness of your divorce journey, you will experience the topography in your own unique way.

When divorce enters our life journey, we all grieve. But our grief journeys are never exactly the same. Despite what you may hear about what the divorce experience is like for someone else, you will encounter it in your own unique way. Be careful about comparing your experience with that of other people.

Are you the leaver or the one who has been left?

When your relationship ends, the split often results in one person being the "leaver" and the other being "left." In the majority of cases, divorce is not equally desired by both spouses. Reports suggest that one person wants the divorce a lot more than the other 75-90 percent of the time.

Regardless of whether you were a leaver or were left, you have your own unique challenges. Many people assume the leaver has an easier time than the person who was left. Yet, that reality is not always true. Ask yourself, where do you fit and what is your experience in this realm?

Remember: Be very tentative in over-generalizing what you might experience based on whether you are the leaver or the left. We do sometimes witness that if you are the left, you may experience more feelings of vulnerability, frustration, and helplessness. Your self-esteem may suffer more than the leaver's, and some people who are left may report having some explosive emotions (see p. 76).

But the experience is not always smooth and easy for the leaver, either. While more likely to feel initial relief, perhaps even some happiness, leavers still experience the high stress that comes with this major life transition. Observation suggests that many leavers, in contrast to those left, experience high stress before the separation and divorce and feelings of guilt after the separation and divorce. So, whether you were a leaver or were left, divorce is often difficult and painful. It just seems that the timing of one's stress levels may be different for each person.

Where you are emotionally and spiritually right now is not where you will be next week, next month or next year. While some circumstances may require your immediate attention, consider taking a "one-day-at-a-time" approach. Doing so allows you to integrate this massive change into your life at your own pace.

This Touchstone invites you to explore some of the unique aspects of your divorce experience—the "influences" on your journey through this wilderness. Remember, I am attempting to help you mourn what you have lost in an effort to eventually help free you to live a meaningful, fulfilling new life. While some people will tell you otherwise, I believe there are times in life we have to go backward before we go forward. As you contemplate and write out your responses in your companion journal, I believe you will discover an increased understanding of the uniqueness of your divorce experience.

Influence #1: The circumstances of the divorce

There are many circumstances that can make each divorce unique. Some couples come to divorce after years of alienation, constant fighting and neglect. The wounds from this kind of history often run very deep and are naturally complex. Perhaps there had been a long-term lack of emotional intimacy, and in many ways, the couple was apart emotionally long before they considered a physical separation. Of course, there are a myriad of ways couples end up divorcing.

You may have felt you still loved your spouse, yet he or she suddenly announced he or she wanted a divorce. In this case you are encountering grief before you are prepared to mourn. Or, perhaps you lived with your spouse for a long time after learning you were no longer loved by him or her. Maybe you realized early on in your marriage that one day it would end; you just didn't know when. Yes, the ending of a relationship, just like the beginning of one, can be a complex and mysterious process.

Perhaps you discovered your spouse was involved in an affair. Maybe you feel betrayed by your spouse. As one person said to me recently, "I felt betrayed in this relationship many times."

Or, perhaps your own involvement in an affair resulted in a separation and divorce.

Maybe you fell more in love with your career than with your spouse, and you drifted apart. Perhaps you became very different people than when you first connected and found that as you grew personally, you grew apart from the relationship. Maybe one or both of you realized you never made a separation from your family of origin that allowed you to be an autonomous individual, and this had made it difficult to engage in or commit to an intimate adult relationship with your spouse.

Maybe you were in an abusive relationship and decided to get out while you could. Or, maybe you were in what is called a "trauma-bonded" relationship, where there was a mixture of intensely positive and negative experiences that create a bond that is almost undissolvable. Maybe you yourself or someone else helped extricate you from the relationship because of concern for your safety and well-being.

Perhaps you experienced a "bounce-back, dangling separation" prior to the divorce. This is where you separate (whether legally, physically or emotionally) but keep getting back together. This happens when one or both partners pretend or deny that the marriage is not really going to end. Then, at some point, one of you discovers the need or desire to finally make a final break.

"It is not a lack of love, but a lack of friendship that makes unhappy marriages."
Friedrich Nietzsche

In my work with hundreds of divorced couples over many years, they have taught me about a multitude of circumstances or problems they feel have contributed to their divorces. These may include lack of intimacy, differences in parenting style, infidelity, growing apart, and boredom—to note just a few. Probably the most common is what I would term a lack of an essential emotional connection. I have had many people say, "I no longer had any passion for the other person" or

"I fell out of love with my spouse." The potential reasons for this changed passion are multiple and complex.

Again, the list of potential circumstances surrounding your unique divorce are almost endless. Regardless of your unique circumstances, the ending of a relationship is a naturally difficult rite of passage to a life that will be very different than before. The great challenge is how you will respond to this life-changing experience. Whether your marriage died a slow death or experienced an unexpected crisis that created an end, whether you were the "leaver" or the "left," you are now faced with a need to mourn what once was.

EXPRESS YOURSELF: Go to *The Transcending Divorce Journal*, p. 32.

Influence #2: Your unique personality

What words would you use to describe yourself? What words would people use to describe you? Are you a serious person? Light-hearted? Quiet? Are you a nurturer? A fixer? Are you a protector?

The point is that whatever your unique personality, rest assured that it will be reflected in your response to the divorce experience and the way you mourn this major life change. For example, if you are quiet by nature, you may express your grief related to your lost dreams quietly. If you tend to be expressive, you may openly express how you feel about your divorce.

How you have responded to other changes, losses and transitions in your life may be consistent with how you respond to the divorce. If you tend to run away from stressful aspects of life, you may have an instinct to do the same thing now. If, however, you have always confronted crisis head on and openly, you may walk right into the center of the wilderness. While grief and the need to mourn is natural, some people allow themselves to mourn more openly than others.

Other aspects of your personality, such as your self-esteem, values, and beliefs, also impact your response to divorce. In addition, any long-term problems with depression or anxiety will probably influence your grief.

EXPRESS YOURSELF: Go to *The Transcending Divorce Journal*, p. 34.

Influence #3: The people in your life

How are the people around you supporting you at this difficult time? Mourning lost relationship dreams requires mourning. Mourning, as I have defined it in this book, requires the outside support of other human beings in order to bring about integration of this major life transition.

Without a stabilizing support system of at least one other person, the odds are that you will have difficulty doing your work of mourning. Healing requires an environment of empathy, caring, acceptance and gentle encouragement. Have your friends and family been supportive to you in ways that help you?

Sometimes other people may think that you have a support system when in fact you don't. For example, you may have some family and friends who sit in judgment of you and are unable to compassionately support you. If so, a vital catalyst to your healing—compassionate others who bear witness to your pain— is missing.

Keep in mind that you may discover some people who have always thought and will always think that divorces should never happen, regardless of the circumstances. They often project that "divorce is a sin" and sit in judgment of you. If at all possible, these are people to avoid. Obviously, instead of offering the support you need, being in their presence will often end up leaving you feeling worse about yourself and your circumstances.

> *"Walking with a friend in the dark is better than walking alone in the light."*
> Helen Keller

You may have some friends and relatives who were supportive prior to the divorce but pulled away soon after. Again, for healing to occur, sound support anchored in compassion, concern and love really needs to be accessible and ongoing.

In contrast, you may have an amazing support system and feel you are wrapped in unconditional love. But even when you have a solid support system in place, you might want to ask yourself, "Am I willing and able to accept the support offered by others?" If you pull in too much, you may end up isolating yourself from the very people who would most like to walk with you on your journey through the wilderness of your divorce.

"I remember how important what I called my 'telephone lifeline' was. It helped me stay balanced at a time of great imbalance. My dear friend, Joanne, was particularly helpful and made certain she talked to me every day."

Mary S.

EXPRESS YOURSELF: Go to *The Transcending Divorce Journal*, p. 37.

Influence #4: Your children

Perhaps you have heard it said that while marriages aren't always forever, parenting is for life. Obviously, when we explore influences on your divorce experience, one of the most important is how your children are impacted by the divorce. Perhaps you don't have children and this is not an influence on your experience. However, if you do, you realize that your children will be a forever link to your ex-spouse. Even in situations of abandonment, there is still a link to a former spouse when children are involved. You are divorcing each other, but I hope you are not divorcing yourself from your children. While the topic of children of divorce is beyond the intended scope of this book, allow me to explore some divorce realities related to children. If you don't have children, feel free to skip to the next influence.

Whether you have young children, teenage children or adult children, you are probably concerned about how your divorce is affecting them and your relationship with them. We would be deceiving ourselves not to recognize that parental divorce is naturally difficult for children, regardless of their age. Fortunately there are many resources available to help alert you to common struggles children of divorce confront at various ages and circumstances. One of my personal favorites is Vicky Lansky's *Divorce Book for Parents* (ISBN 0-916772-48-5), which explores a multitude of topics that you may find helpful. You will find information ranging from breaking the news and age-related behavior to anticipate to custody issues, single-parenting, and insights from other parents.

Yes, just as divorce brings losses and the need to mourn into your life, it does the same for your children. I'm often asked, "Does divorce cause long-term problems for children?" While there have been a multitude of different studies that have looked at this issue, the findings seem to conclude that a *minority* of children do develop long-term emotional, behavioral, social, or academic problems. And even some who appeared to be doing well during the initial separation may go on to experience difficulties later. However, and this is a BIG and IMPORTANT however, the majority, when they receive adequate and compassionate support, are NOT TROUBLED with lasting problems, and some even develop greater psychological strength following the divorce.

> *"We are divorced, we are friends, and we are good parents."*
>
> Sarah Ferguson

The really good news is that recent research has helped us understand why some children emerge from the divorce experience relatively unscathed while others develop long-term problems. By making use of the information available, you have the opportunity to help your children survive and thrive in the face of divorce.

It is so very important to remember that even the most caring parents don't completely have it together when divorce becomes a part of their life journey. Keep in mind that all change usually starts with chaos. It is naturally difficult to be totally available and supportive to your children's emotional and spiritual needs at this time. Please don't be too hard on yourself if you make some missteps while you are in this wilderness experience. Your sincerity, consideration and love will make up for some of the difficult patches you encounter.

EXPRESS YOURSELF: Go to *The Transcending Divorce Journal*, p. 40.

Influence #5: Your gender

Your gender may not only influence your divorce transition and grief experience, but also how others relate to you at this time. Let's briefly explore some of those potential differences and you can then determine if they have any application to yourself.

While this is certainly not always true, men are more often encouraged and expected to "be strong" and restrained in their emotional expressions around loss and grief. Sometimes, men have more difficulty allowing themselves the move toward painful feelings than women do.

Women sometimes have a hard time expressing feelings of protest and anger. By contrast, men may be quicker to respond with a variety of explosive emotions. And because many men are conditioned to be self-sufficient, they often have difficulty accepting outside support.

WARNING: We must be very careful about generalizations related to these gender differences. Sometimes too much is made of the differences between genders and not enough is made of the human capacity to grieve and mourn. The need to mourn divorce loss is essential regardless of gender.

Research Findings on Gender

One study concluded that women face more stressors due to divorce than men regarding income, social activity and single parenthood. This has resulted in some researchers concluding that women suffer more as a result of divorce. Yet, in other findings women actually fare better in terms of divorce adjustment than do men. For women, a sense of growth in self-esteem appears to result from the divorce, and the effects of these changes appear long-lasting.

Despite popular stereotypes, men suffer the pain of divorce as much as women, and seem to feel many of the same emotions, although they may be expressed in different ways.

Whether you are male or female, you need to mourn this major life change in your own unique way. You need to feel connected to people around you (both male and female) who help you feel understood and supported. In many ways, your healing and transformation begin when you realize you share a similar journey to that of many other women and men.

EXPRESS YOURSELF: Go to *The Transcending Divorce Journal*, p. 42.

Influence #6: Your cultural/ethnic background

Your cultural and ethnic background can be an important influence on how you experience and express the grief related to your divorce. Sometimes it is difficult for modern-day North Americans to articulate what their cultural/ethnic background is. "My mother is half English, a little Irish with some German," you might say. "And my father is from a strong Italian family." So what does that make you? And how does this mixture influence your divorce experience?

When I say culture, I mean the values, rules (spoken and unspoken), and traditions that guide you and your family. Education and political beliefs are also aspects of your cultural background (religion, too, but we'll get to that next). Often these values, rules, traditions and beliefs have been handed down generation to generation and are shaped by the countries or areas of the world your family originally came from.

In some cultures divorce is seen as something that should never happen regardless of circumstances. In other words, you marry for life and if you don't stay married, you are shunned and ostracized. Divorce is even illegal in the Philippines and Malta, and was only recently legalized in Chile. In contrast, some cultures are more open to the realities of divorce and support people through the experience. What comes to mind when you reflect on how your cultural/ethnic background might be influencing your divorce experience?

EXPRESS YOURSELF: Go to *The Transcending Divorce Journal*, p. 43.

Influence #7: Your religious or spiritual background

Your personal belief system can have a tremendous impact on your divorce experience. You may discover that your religious or spiritual life is initiated, changed, deepened or renewed in some way as a result of your divorce journey. Or you may well find yourself questioning your beliefs as part of your work as you mourn your marriage.

When experiencing divorce, some people may feel very close to God or a Higher Power, while others may feel more distant and angry. You may find yourself asking questions such as, "Why has this happened to me?" or "How could what started out so good, turn so bad?" You may not find the answers to all of your questions about faith and spirituality. However, that doesn't mean you don't need to ask the questions. I find that *why* questions often precede *how* questions. In other words, "Why did this happen?" often precedes "How will I survive it?"

The word "faith" means to believe in something for which there is no proof. For some people, faith means believing in and following a set of religious tenets. For others, faith is belief in God, a spiritual presence, or a force that is greater than we are.

Mistakenly, some people think that being "strong in faith" means you can bypass the need to mourn your divorce. If you buy into this misconception, you will set yourself up to grieve internally but not mourn externally. *Having faith does not mean you do not need to mourn your lost relationship, hopes and dreams. Having faith means having the courage to mourn your lost relationship, hopes and dreams.*

As previously noted under Influence #3, "The People in Your Life," you will probably cross paths with someone who projects that no one should ever get a divorce and that it is a "sin."

Again, I suggest you try to keep your distance from these people and seek out support from people who are not judgmental, but instead permit you to place your own spiritual or religious meaning on this experience.

With the divorce journey comes a "search for meaning" (we will explore this on page 127). You will naturally find yourself reevaluating your life based on this major life transition. You will probably benefit from finding someone who is able and willing to listen to you as you explore your religious/spiritual values, question your attitude toward life, and renew your resources for living. This process takes time and patience, and it may lead to potential changes in your values, beliefs and view of the world.

EXPRESS YOURSELF: Go to *The Transcending Divorce Journal*, p. 44.

Influence #8: Other changes, crises or stresses in your life right now

What else is going on in your life right now? As noted under Touchstone One, there is often a ripple effect of additional losses and stresses that impact you in a multitude of ways during and after a divorce. While some people tend to think of divorce as a single event, it is actually a process that involves a multitude of changes and stresses. To mention a few, there are often changes in your normal routine, finances, social life, personal identity, family identity, and dreams and goals.

Other people in your life may be sick or in need of some kind of help right now. You may have children or elderly parents (or both!) to care for. You may have a number of commitments, yet

"You need chaos in your soul to give birth to a dancing star."

Friedrich Nietzsche

little time and energy for all the demands you are experiencing. Maybe you have some health problems or have lost the comfort of living in a home you lived in for some time. Perhaps you are limited to weekend visits with your children. No, divorce does not take place as a single life event and is usually accompanied by additional changes, crises, and stresses.

Whatever your specific situation, I'm sure that your divorce grief is not the only stress in your life right now. And the more intense and numerous the stresses in your life, the more overwhelmed you may feel at times.

Very few people are prepared for the degree to which their lives are disrupted and changed by divorce. While many understand that there will be change and stress, my experience is that most people underestimate them. Also, you may not realize how disorienting and confusing the changes in daily routines and habits will be.

As previously noted, all major life change starts with chaos. That is why you will want to pay special attention to the importance of nurturing yourself (see p. 133) and reaching out for and accepting help (see p. 159). Yes, you probably are under loads of stress and many changes right now. But remember, you will survive and go on to thrive. Be patient and self-nurturing during this time of massive change in your life journey.

EXPRESS YOURSELF: Go to *The Transcending Divorce Journal*, p. 46.

Influence #9: Your physical health

How you feel physically will have a significant impact on how you cope with the stresses and changes you are experiencing. Obviously, stress and transition cause physiological changes to your body. Be aware that you may be more vulnerable to viruses and other illnesses right now.

Lack of care of your body will add more stress to your life. If you are tired and eating poorly, your coping skills will be diminished. If you are self-treating stress with alcohol or drugs, you are adding even more stress on your body. If you have a preexisting medical condition, you may notice that it is impacted or complicated by the current stress you are experiencing.

If you are physically sick, your bodily symptoms may be just as pressing, if not more pressing, than your emotional and spiritual ones. Some of the self-care considerations outlined in this book to combat stress are physiological in nature (see p. 136). The importance of using the techniques cannot be overemphasized. You only have one body; be gentle, kind and loving to it.

We will discuss more on the care of your body under Touchstone Seven, p. 133. For now, bear in mind that taking care of yourself physically is one of the best things you can do to lay a foundation that is centered on self-care and self-compassion at this stressful time in your life.

EXPRESS YOURSELF: Go to *The Transcending Divorce Journal*, p. 47.

Influence #10: Your financial health

How is your financial health? Not only are you physically and emotionally vulnerable during this time in your life, you are economically vulnerable. You may be in intensive care related to your economic health. Some who get divorced have plenty of resources, while others have literally no means to support themselves.

Perhaps you need counsel on how to safeguard what financial resources you do have. Perhaps you have had to file paperwork to ensure you receive spousal and child support. Maybe you need to learn to develop and operate on a budget for the first time in your life.

"A lot of people have asked me how short I am. Since my last divorce, I think I'm about $100,000 short."

Mickey Rooney

Or, like many divorced persons I have worked with, you may have never felt a need to strategically plan for your financial future. Appropriate financial planning based on your current situation cannot be overemphasized. Your quality of life and future peace of mind will depend upon it. A vital step is to safeguard any assets you have at this time.

The reality is that some people really struggle financially after a divorce. One major study found that, on average, women experience a 15 to 30 percent drop in their income following divorce. Sometimes getting credit after a divorce can be a challenge. Perhaps you have had to sell your family home and are essentially starting over.

In sum, you will now have to take financial responsibility for yourself, and with that comes stress. Even if you feel fortunate in this area, you might be wise to get a financial check-up and counsel that will help you understand your situation and plan accordingly. Fortunately, there are many resources available that can help you cope with your financial present and future.

EXPRESS YOURSELF: Go to *The Transcending Divorce Journal*, p. 48.

Other Factors Influencing Your Divorce Experience

What else is shaping your unique divorce experience? There are probably other factors, large and small, that are influencing your journey right now. What are they? I invite you to think about them and to write about them in your companion journal.

EXPRESS YOURSELF: Go to *The Transcending Divorce Journal*, p. 49.

This Touchstone has encouraged you to explore some of the unique aspects of your divorce experience—the "influences" of your journey through the wilderness. Again, the purpose of doing this is to help you mourn what you have lost in an effort to eventually help you go forward to a life filled with meaning and purpose. I am honored to companion you on this journey.

Next, I will lead you into an exploration of some of the feelings you may be encountering during this time in your life. I have discovered that an important part of integrating divorce into your life involves listening to and attending to your inner voice, then giving expression to those thoughts and feelings as you experience them. While it may sound simplistic, I have come to know that we all have to "feel it to heal it." In the next chapter we will discuss some of these common and varied feelings.

Touchstone Four

Explore Your Feelings of Loss

"Today I woke up in a well of overwhelming emotions. Feeling disconnected, I got my feet out of bed and put one foot in front of another. It is like I'm lost in a wilderness of emotions. I'm scared, alone, and feel like there is an invisible blanket between the world and me."

M. Johnson

Stepping into the wilderness of your many feelings is an important and sacred part of your life right now. It is my experience that we cannot heal what we cannot or do not allow ourselves to feel. Being in the wilderness of your emotions invites you to get to know your authentic self and feel the depth of your broken heart.

Divorce creates profound disruption in almost all areas of your life. It exposes internal and external conflicts. It challenges all that you know about yourself. This journey rocks the complete foundation of your entire being. Divorce is synonymous with disruption, chaos, and change—all of which bring a multitude of conflicting emotions. Taking ownership of your wilderness emotions is the only way to eventually re-orient and transcend this major life transition. And as your companion, I urge you to remember: Out of the darkness will come light! Be patient, be steadfast, and be self-compassionate as we explore this important Touchstone.

The Importance of Experiencing and Expressing Your Feelings

As strange as your emotions may seem, they are a true expression of where you are right now. Rather than deny or feel victimized by your feelings, I want to help you learn to recognize and learn from them. Naming the feelings and acknowledging them are the first steps to befriending them. Yes, in my experience, it's actually this process of becoming friendly with your feelings that will help you heal, or become whole again. Perhaps it is helpful to think of feelings as our teachers. All transcendence starts with awareness of our feelings. So, I invite you to be open to your teachers!

Now some might say, "What is the point of experiencing and expressing feelings if they don't change anything?" I get this question often from people going through a divorce.

It's true that experiencing and talking about your feelings does not change what you are going through. However, self-expression does have the capacity to change you and the way you see and experience the world around you. Putting your feelings into words gives them meaning and shape. Putting your thoughts and feelings into the world outside yourself helps you begin to feel whole again. Remember, you have been torn apart. Allow me the honor of trying to help you reconstruct yourself.

To express means, in part, to press out, to make known, to reveal. When we have strong feelings and we don't express, we risk exploding. I don't want you to explode and disintegrate. And the danger of such an explosion and disintegration is high if you repress instead of express. Expression actually allows you a kind of freedom—the freedom to recognize and integrate your emotions in their fullest form.

This expression of feelings that brings release from the risk of explosion and disintegration even has a fancy term: *catharsis*. The beauty of this process is that you don't even need to understand what you are feeling in order to express it. You will have time down the line to sort out the texture of your many feelings and explore their origins. For now, let's just create an opportunity for you to befriend whatever thoughts and feelings you are having.

Catharsis

A technique used to relieve tension and anxiety by bringing repressed feelings and fears to consciousness.

My hope is that this Touchstone will help you see how natural your many thoughts, feelings and behaviors are. I have companioned thousands of divorced people, and they have taught me about this journey. I have also walked this walk myself. Rest assured that whatever your thoughts and feelings, while in one sense completely unique to you, they are also usually a common response to divorce.

Questions throughout this section of your companion journal will encourage you to see if a particular feeling I am describing is, or has been, a part of your personal experience.

Your journal is one place to describe your experience and familiarize yourself with various dimensions of your unique journey—to tell your story. As you work through this life-changing experience, you will be working through the story of your life at this difficult time. As you do this work, remember that there is life after divorce, and your grief work is a vital part of the beginning of your new life. Also, keep in mind that although you may not have experienced some of these thoughts and feelings described in this chapter, you may in the future. In addition, these dimensions of potential feelings may be part of your experience, but they don't always unfold neatly in an orderly and predictable way.

Following a discussion of each dimension of divorce grief is a brief statement entitled "A Look Back." These statements are to help orient you to the words those in divorce grief commonly use to describe each dimension.

Now allow me to help you take a closer look at some of the feelings you might experience in your divorce journey:

Shock, Numbness, Denial, and Disbelief

The first reaction for many people facing divorce loss is shock and disbelief. As 43-year-old Bill stated, "I thought we had a pretty good marriage. Some people even told us we were meant for each other. Then, last week she comes home and tells me she is unhappy, has been for a long time and wants out. I keep thinking I'll wake up...I can't believe this is happening."

Bill is not alone in his initial reaction to his new reality. "It feels like a dream," people in early divorce grief often say. "I feel like I might wake up and none of this will have happened." They also say things like, "I was there, but yet I really wasn't. It was like I was outside of myself looking in."

There are times when information we receive is so overwhelming that we become, for a period of time, incapable of feeling. We have a term for it: *psychic numbing.* This frequently occurs if you are the one who is left. While the initial shock may be somewhat easier for those of you who made the decision to leave (or for couples who mutually decide it is time to end the relationship) and for those somewhat prepared for this reality, the ending is still painful and can result in aspects of shock no matter what the circumstances.

> *"Being divorced is like being hit by a Mack truck. If you live through it, you start looking very carefully to the right and to the left."*
> Jean Kerr

Thank goodness for shock, numbness and disbelief! These are not only common initial responses, but also helpful, if they do not continue for too long. Some people also use the words "dazed" and "stunned" to describe their experience.

These anesthetized conditions are nature's way of temporarily protecting you from the full reality of what confronts you. They allow you to stall, to slow things down somewhat. They help insulate you psychologically until you are more able to tolerate what you don't want to believe. In essence, these muted feelings serve as a "temporary timeout" or a "psychological shock absorber."

Especially when you first learn about the beginning of the end of your marriage, your emotions need time to catch up with what your mind has been told. On one level, you know you heard the word divorce. But on other, deeper levels, you are not yet able or willing to truly believe it. This mixture of shock, numbness, and disbelief acts as an anesthetic pushing away overwhelming emotions. The pain exists, but you may not experience it fully. What feelings you do allow in are diffused and let in very slowly, in small doses.

For many people a physiological component also accompanies feelings of shock. Your autonomic nervous system is affected and may cause heart palpitations, queasiness, stomach pain, and dizziness. This often occurs if you are the one left, after the leaver says that he or she is going. You may find yourself hysterically crying, fainting, having angry outbursts, or even laughing. These are all normal and "survival-oriented" responses in the face of a new reality—the end of your marriage. During this time of shock, you may not remember some of the specific words being spoken to you. Your mind is blocking; it hears but does not listen.

Denial is often one of the most misunderstood aspects of the divorce journey. Temporarily, denial, like shock and numbness, is a great gift. It helps you survive. However, your denial, if part of your experience, should soften over time as you acknowledge the reality of the divorce. While denial is helpful—even necessary—early on, ongoing denial clearly blocks the path to healing. If you continue to deny the end of your marriage, eventually this becomes self-defeating and self-destructive. If you cannot eventually acknowledge that your marriage is over, you cannot mourn the loss and move forward with your life.

In my experience, denial often goes on at one level of awareness while acknowledgment of the reality of the end of the relationship goes on at another level. Your mind may approach and retreat from the reality of the divorce over and over again as you try to embrace and integrate what this means for your life. This back-and-forth process is normal. I describe this process as "evading and encountering." How long this back-and-forth dance lasts will vary, depending on the timing, unique circumstances and severity of the shock involved. If you find you cannot get past the need to deny, allow me to gently suggest you might find it helpful to talk to a professional counselor with experience in divorce transition.

A Look Back:
"It was like I was in a box and I couldn't get out of it. Part of me knew what was happening, but I just didn't want to believe it. I let it in a little at a time or I think I might have died of a broken heart." – a divorced woman

Self-care guidelines

A critical point to realize is that shock, denial, numbness, and disbelief are not experiences you try to prevent yourself from having—at least not in the early part of your wilderness journey. Instead, be thankful that this shock absorber is available at a time when you need it most.

Be compassionate with yourself, particularly if news of your divorce came to you suddenly and unexpectedly. Allow for this instinctive form of self-protection. This dimension of grief provides a much-needed, yet temporary, means of survival. You can push the pain away for a while, but the cloudy ache comes back, reminding you that all is not well.

A vital self-care principle during this time is to reach out to caring friends, family, and caregivers you trust. When you are in shock, your instinctive response is to have other people care for you. Let them. Let yourself be nurtured. If you have younger children, allow others to help support and care for them right now.

Accepting support does not mean being totally passive and doing nothing for yourself, though. Actually, having people completely overdo for you is usually not helpful. Given appropriate support and understanding, you will find value in doing some things for yourself. In other words, don't allow anyone to do for you what you want to do for yourself. (WARNING: Auto accident rates double for people during the first six months after separation. Be very careful driving when you are in the throes of shock. Remember, you are under-responsive to outside stimuli like red lights and stop signs. I don't want anything happening to you. After all, you have enough on your plate to cope with right now.)

Remember that a few well-intentioned yet misguided people may try to have you prematurely "overcome" your denial and "face the facts." They might make comments such as, "You just have to admit what has happened and move on." While your ultimate healing and eventual transcendence does require acknowledging the reality of your divorce, this period of shock and numbness is probably not the time to embrace the full depth of your life changes. If others insist on "making you face the reality" without respecting your need to dose yourself, try as best you can to ignore or avoid them. Then, seek out the one-third of people you know who will be empathetic helpers (see p. 161 for the "Rule of Thirds").

EXPRESS YOURSELF: Go to *The Transcending Divorce Journal*, p. 52.

Disorganization and Confusion

A thirty-two-year-old newly divorced woman once described her experience in this way: "My mind keeps jumping around from thought to thought. I keep starting to do one thing, and then right in the middle of it, I start doing something else. To say I'm confused and disorganized is an understatement."

Perhaps the most isolating and frightening part of the divorce journey is this sense of disorganization and confusion that often comes with the experience. This dimension often gives rise to what I call the "going crazy syndrome." Many people going through divorce have said to me, "I think I'm going crazy." That is because the thoughts and behaviors during this time are different from what you normally experience. If you feel disorganized and confused, know that you are not going crazy. You are experiencing grief and the need to mourn.

The divorce journey often results in experiences of restlessness, agitation, impatience, and ongoing confusion and disorganization. It's like being in the middle of a wild, rushing river where you can't get a grasp on anything. Or, to use the wilderness metaphor, you are in the middle of a dark forest, and no matter which way you turn, you cannot seem to find your way out.

"Divorce puts you on the edge of sanity."

Abigail Trafford

You may express disorganization and confusion in your inability to complete tasks. You may start to do something but never finish. You may feel forgetful and ineffective, especially early in the morning and late at night, when fatigue and lethargy are most prominent. Disconnected thoughts may race through your mind and a multitude of strong emotions may be overwhelming. This is also usually accompanied by what is called *anhedonia*—the inability to find joy in things that previously brought you joy.

Other common experiences during this time include difficulties with eating and sleeping. You may experience a loss of appetite, or you may find yourself overeating. Even when you do eat, you may be unable to taste the food. Having trouble falling asleep, disruption of your sleep during the night, and early-morning awakening are also common during this dimension of your divorce journey.

Another way to understand this dimension is through a discussion of the five domains in which stress impacts your life: physical, emotional, cognitive, social and spiritual. The stress of divorce affects each of these areas of your life:

- *Physically*: your body feels exhausted.

- *Emotionally*: your feelings are intense and overwhelming.

- *Cognitively*: your mind has trouble concentrating and staying focused.

- *Socially*: your relationships require energy that you don't have.

- *Spiritually*: you may question the meaning and purpose of your life.

If you are feeling stressed in all five dimensions, it is no wonder you encounter aspects of disorganization and confusion!

And finally, keep in mind that whenever we as human beings experience major life transitions, we encounter disorganization, confusion and chaos on the pathway to any kind of reorganization. While it may seem strange, it has helped many people I have companioned on the divorce journey to remind themselves that disorganization and confusion are actually steppingstones on the path toward healing and transformation.

Self-care guidelines

If you find that disorganization and confusion are, or have been, part of your journey, please realize you are not alone. As a matter of fact, I'd be concerned if you didn't have some features of disorganization and confusion when you are going through a divorce. So, remember—you are not crazy. You simply have special needs and are mourning a major life change.

A Look Back

"It was like I was lost in a maze. Every way I turned I couldn't find any sense of direction. I had to go slow and be very patient with myself. My confusion did soften over time as I got support, but for a while it was really frightening to feel so disoriented."
– a divorced man

The thoughts, feelings and behaviors of this dimension do not come all at once. They are often experienced in a wave-like fashion. You may need to talk and cry for long periods of time. At other times, you may just need to go to exile and spend some time alone.

Try not to interpret what you are thinking and feeling. Just think and feel it. Allowing yourself to let in whatever you are experiencing is actually one of the best ways to remain in an active healing process. Don't get defensive with yourself and shut down. If you want disorientation and confusion to soften, the only cushion for them to fall on is your awareness and expression. Give your disorientation the attention it deserves and demands.

When you feel disoriented, talk to someone who will be supportive and understanding. Sometimes when you talk, you may not think you make much sense. And you may not. But talking it out can still be self-clarifying, even at a subconscious level.

Again, to integrate grief that comes with divorce loss, mourning is a requirement. I hope you have at least one person whom you feel understands and will not judge you. That person must be patient and attentive because you may revisit aspects of your divorce over and over again as you befriend your grief. He or she must be genuinely interested in understanding you. If you are trying to talk about your disorganization and confusion and the person with whom you are speaking doesn't want to listen, find someone who will better meet your needs.

WARNING: It is not only the confusing "down" feelings you want to embrace, but also the "up" feelings that help counter your sad, depressed mood. Positive thoughts and feelings such as hopefulness, peacefulness, inner-strength, courage and confidence should be given your focused attention as well. In the midst of your chaos, look for these and you may be surprised what you discover along the path!

Oh, one more important warning based on my experience with thousands of people going through divorce transition. Whenever possible, avoid making any impulsive decisions such as quitting your job, moving to another community or rebounding into another relationship too quickly. Because of the judgment-making difficulties that naturally come with this part of the journey, ill-timed, premature decisions might result in more loss on top of loss. Go slow and be patient with yourself. Sometimes divorced people unconsciously try to push away pain and confusion by moving to action too quickly. Remember one of my favorite mantras and repeat it to yourself: "There are no rewards for speed!"

EXPRESS YOURSELF: Go to *The Transcending Divorce Journal*, p. 55.

Anxiety, Panic and Fear

"I started having mini-panic attacks and felt scared about my future," said 51-year-old Roger. "I had financial worries and questioned if my kids would reject me and ever want to see me again. The panic and fear I felt were very real."

Feelings of anxiety, panic and fear also may be a part of your experience. Anxiety is often inevitable during times of major disruption, where what has been familiar is being replaced with an uncertain future, emotions are overwhelming, decisions are pressing, and new day-to-day problems require action. Sometimes, anxiety can result in panic, which will produce symptoms such as a racing pulse, shortness of breath, tightened chest, and profuse perspiration.

You may ask yourself, "Am I going to be OK?" " Will I survive this" "Will my future have some meaning and purpose?" "Will I be alone the rest of my life?" These questions are natural. Your sense of security has been threatened, so you are naturally anxious and fearful.

As your head and heart encounter your new, uncertain sense of future, it may bring some anxiety, panic and fear into your awareness. Feelings like this often elicit thoughts about "going crazy." If you begin to think you are "abnormal," your level of fear may also increase. So, remind yourself—you are *not* abnormal, you are going through a major life transition.

Yes, right now you may feel a new sense of vulnerability unlike anything you might have experienced before. You may be frightened by your inability to concentrate because of your fear and worry. For many people going through divorce, financial challenges compound feelings of anxiety.

Your sleep might be affected by anxiety and fear at this time. Fears of overwhelming, painful thoughts and feelings that can come up in dreams or nightmares may cause you difficulty with sleeping. Or, as some people report, you may be afraid of being alone in your home or sleeping by yourself. Again, these are natural, but usually temporary, ways that fear can be a part of your divorce grief.

"Only when we are no longer afraid do we begin to live."
Dorothy Thompson

While unpleasant, anxiety, panic and fear are often normal elements of this experience. The good news is that expressing them can help make them feel more tolerable. And knowing that they are temporary may help you during this trying time.

A Look Back
"Among other things, I was afraid of being hurt again, abandoned again, being alone, having to work all the time, going broke and not being forgiven by God. For a while I was paralyzed by fear, but the good news is that the fear goes away. It required me to have courage and take action."
– a divorced woman

Self-care guidelines

First, remember that anxiety and fear actually serve a good purpose. They alert you to things that need your attention and eventual action. They remind you that you may have to play a part in solving a problem or addressing a challenge. For example, if you are having panic attacks that immobilize you, you will probably have to get some outside help. You might have to make some changes to reduce your stress wherever possible. If you fear losing your home, you might have to adjust your budget or work more. If your kids are hostile towards you, you may have to sit down with them and have a heart-to-heart talk.

Also, remember that without fear, you might not discover you have some courage. In part, courage is the capacity to understand your fears are normal, yet face them anyway—to have faith, if you will!

So, if anxiety, panic and fear are a part of your journey right now, commit to yourself to talk to someone who will be understanding and supportive. Not talking about these feelings makes them so much more powerful and potentially destructive.

I often find that if divorced people don't acknowledge their fears, they find themselves retreating from other people and from the world in general. Please don't become a prisoner in your own home. If you repress your anxiety, you may discover these feelings are now repressing you. I plead with you—do not let this happen to you. And if you are having full-blown panic attacks, please make an appointment and go get help as soon as possible.

Remember, you can't address challenges if you are too overwhelmed with anxiety to function. Take action now to reduce your anxiety to a survivable level immediately. As you do this, remember that all decisions you are forced to make right now don't necessarily have to be permanent ones. In fact, making some temporary decisions will help you have a little more sense of control in your life.

Consider using some deep breathing exercises (see p. 147 for a description of autogenic breathing exercises) to help you with your anxiety. Write in the companion journal to help you sort out your thoughts, feelings and options. Journaling is a powerful way to help you track your progress. It also allows you to get thoughts on paper instead of holding them in your head, where they are more likely to keep getting in your way throughout the day and night. Also, remember that building in a regular exercise program can do wonders to help with anxiety (see p. 136 for more on physical self-care). Of course, one additional possibility is going to see a good counselor (see p. 163 for considerations when selecting a counselor).

EXPRESS YOURSELF: Go to *The Transcending Divorce Journal*, p. 57.

Explosive Emotions

"I wasn't just mad, I was over-the-top angry," said 28-year-old Sharon. "When my husband walked out, I felt abandoned and alone. I yelled and cried until I emptied myself out. It was like he just all of a sudden wanted out of a marriage I had poured my heart into."

The many losses that divorce brings about naturally provide fuel for various explosive emotions. As you come to acknowledge the reality that your marriage is ending, emotions of protest often call out for expression. Anger, hate, blame, terror, resentment, rage, and even jealousy are explosive emotions that may be part of your experience. For some, unfamiliar feelings of vindictiveness and bitterness may feel like they are taking you over. Your married friends and family members may not understand how palpable these emotions are if they have never experienced the end of a love relationship.

I have found that it helps to understand that all of these explosive feelings are, fundamentally, a form of *protest*. We know that it is actually psycho-biologically instinctive in the face of loss and massive change to protest—to dislike your new reality and want to change it in some way.

Just as an infant cries out in the face of loss, you too, may protest, "How could this happen? This isn't fair! I hate this!" You may direct these emotions at your spouse, at the situation, or at anyone who is nearby. You may become occupied with old hurts, reliving them in ways that feel like yesterday. You may even feel a deep, visceral anger inside of you. You may feel raw and exposed. You might even feel frightened by some of your own explosive emotions.

Protest is an instinctive attempt to get back what you lost that you value.

Unfortunately, our society doesn't understand how normal and necessary these feelings can be. No, you don't want to get "stuck" in them or have them lead to outward or inward destruction, but you are human and capable of explosive emotions. Sad to say, some people around you will probably try to convince you that demonstrating any kind of emotional hurt is wrong. The message is often that you are "out of control" and should try to "keep it together."

When you are protesting, people around you may get upset out of a sense of helplessness. As already noted, the intensity of your own emotions may upset you (particularly if you grew

"Anger ventilated often hurries toward forgiveness, and concealed often hardens into revenge."

Edward G. Bulwer-Lytton

up in a family where anger was seen as a "bad" emotion). Still, you must give yourself permission to feel whatever you feel and to express those feelings. Yes, anger needs to be expressed in healthy ways. That will not happen if you collaborate with well-intentioned but misinformed people who try to shut you down. If that happens, your body, mind and spirit will probably be damaged in the process.

Watch out for people who may try to tell you that explosive emotions are not logical. "Anger won't change anything," they might say. "You are better off without him, so get over it." You might find yourself buying into this rational thinking. That's just the problem—thinking is logical; feeling is not. Protest emotions are often an expression from the depths of your soul.

Another problem is that many people oversimplify explosive emotions by talking only about anger. Actually, you may experience a whole range of intense feelings such as those noted above. Underneath these emotions are usually feelings of pain, helplessness, frustration, fear, and hurt. If you discover people who allow you to mourn, you will be able to explore these primary emotions and they will soften. You will experience perturbation! (Go back for a moment and re-read about the concept of perturbation on p. 32.)

Some people who write about divorce transition make an important distinction between what can be referred to as "old anger" versus "new anger." Understanding this distinction might be helpful to you. "Old anger" is about situations you can no longer change. For example, you cannot change past hurts, injustices, frustrations, and betrayals. It is thought that before you can free yourself to go forward in your "new life," you will have to soothe or integrate this old anger.

"New anger" relates to definable situations in the here and now. Common examples include your former spouse being late with child-support payments and your ex sabotaging your relationship with your children. These are situations you may be able to do something about, but they are very different than "old anger." Also, there may be some new anger you can't do much about that will zap your energy if you keep thinking you can. Examples here would include things like whom your ex dates and how she or he lives life from now on. The thought is that carrying anger about these kinds of situations will only serve to make you miserable. Actually, the way to deal with new anger is the same way you deal with old anger: try to soothe it and integrate it in ways that no longer have control over you.

If explosive emotions are part of your journey (and they aren't for everyone), be aware that you have two avenues for expression—outward or inward. The outward avenue leads to eventual healing and transformation; the inward does not. Keeping your explosive emotions inside often leads to low self-esteem, depression, anxiety disorders, guilt, physical complaints and sometimes even persistent thoughts of self-destruction. (Please see the important discussion of suicidal thoughts and feelings on p. 111.)

> *"Holding on to anger is like grasping a hot coal with the intent of throwing it at someone else; you are the one who gets burned."*
> Buddha

Keeping in mind the important concept of perturbation, you should expect your explosive emotions to lessen in intensity and duration as you mourn your divorce transition. The key is often related to finding others who will help you understand what you are feeling and allow you to befriend your underlying feelings of hurt, pain and loss. There is not much point in clinging to anger over things you cannot change.

Remember—you can't go around your divorce grief, or over it, or under it—you must go through it. I hope that as you journey through grief you will be surrounded by people who understand, support and love you and will help you explore your explosive emotions without judging you or trying to stifle you.

REALITY: : Leavers may not express protest emotions because they feel guilty. Those who are left may not express anger because they fear the other person will not come back if they do. However, whether you are the leaver or the left, if you have protest emotions at some point, they will have to be expressed if they are going to be healed and integrated into your life.

Self-care guidelines

The place to start is with the realization that it's okay to feel explosive emotions. They are, without doubt, part of being human. You may have grown up, as many people did, with the belief that it is not okay to feel angry. Now you have to unlearn and relearn that it is instinctive to protest when loss and change enters your life. (Tip: It's much easier to realize this in your head than it is to actually do it in your daily life.) If you have repressed protest emotions, you don't just flip a switch and start expressing them.

So, my hope is that I have gently reminded you that explosive emotions must be expressed, not repressed or, worse yet, totally denied. Don't prescribe these feelings for yourself but do be alert for them. You will need a supportive listener who can tolerate, encourage and validate your explosive emotions without judging, retaliating, or arguing with you. The comforting presence of someone who cares

A Look Back:
"For months I felt like a raging bull. I was consumed by anger. I yelled. I screamed. I even threw things a few times. Then I started going to a support group, and they helped me realize I couldn't let her decision to bail out of the marriage control me so much. The group helped me feel my pain and hurt, but then I started to create a new life. I got motivated to have a good life and now I'm happy to report I do." – a divorced man

about you will help you seek continued self-understanding of your divorce experience.

Be aware, though, of the difference between the right to feel explosive emotions and the right to act out these emotions in harmful ways. It's okay, sometimes even necessary, to feel angry. However, you have to learn as many constructive ways of expressing anger as possible (for example, physical exercise, even humor sometimes). If you hurt others or yourself or destroy property, the people who care about you will need to set limits on your behavior.

A few other key principles to keep in mind:

• Protest emotions are, at times, instinctive responses intended to spur you to constructive action.

• Protest emotions are sometimes a reaction to a sense of injustice, whether real or perceived.

• Protest emotions can often indicate underlying feelings of pain, helplessness, frustration, fear and hurt. Listen to your protest emotions and consider exploring what may be beneath the surface.

• The integration of protest emotions will eventually allow you to move forward while always remembering your past.

• The experiencing of protest emotions sometimes indicates a need to explore forgiveness or to try to seek atonement for wrongs you may have done to someone you once loved deeply.

So, keep reminding yourself that explosive emotions are not good or bad, right or wrong. They just are. They are your feelings, and they are symptoms of an injury that needs nurturing, not judging. Paradoxically, the way to diminish explosive emotions is to experience them, even if they seem irrational to you.

EXPRESS YOURSELF: Go to *The Transcending Divorce Journal*, p. 59.

Guilt, Regret, Self-blame, Shame, Rejection, Worthlessness and Failure

Thirty-nine-year-old Brad said, "While I initiated the separation, I felt like she rejected me a long time before I moved out. We didn't talk much, and she didn't show any interest in me. Maybe I didn't try hard enough…I feel like such a failure."

This constellation of potential feelings is a common part of the emotional rollercoaster of the divorce experience. Again, remember that some of these feelings may apply for you while others may not. While each of these emotions has unique aspects, I have pulled them together here to introduce them for your reflection.

When the initial shock of what you are going through wears off, you may find yourself with some of the following questions: "What could I have done differently?" "Where did we go wrong?" "Why do I feel so rejected?" "Am I a total failure or what?"

Similarly, some divorced people experience a serious case of the "if onlys": "If only I had been more attentive to her and pursued my career less." "If only we had spent more quality time together." "If only we hadn't had the kids so soon, so we could have gotten to know each other better." "If only we had more things in common."

"Divorce is the psychological equivalent of a triple coronary bypass. After such a monumental assault on the heart, it takes years to amend all the habits and attitudes that led up to it."

Mary Kay Blakely

When a relationship you once had warm, loving feelings about comes to an end, it is natural to think about actions you could have taken to change the outcome. If you find yourself experiencing some "if onlys," be compassionate with yourself. What a genuine human response in the face of loss and hoped-for dreams!

If you are feeling guilty, you might find it helpful to reflect on the distinction between "real" guilt and "false" guilt. Real guilt is when you experience genuine guilt in some way, shape or form. For example, perhaps you feel real guilt for having had an affair while you were married. Perhaps you feel real guilt because you were abusive to your spouse in some way. Perhaps you feel real guilt because you now see that you did not give the time or attention the relationship needed if it was to have any chance of surviving.

In contrast, false guilt is when you internalize societal guilt surrounding your divorce. This false guilt is often projected from the inside to the outside and is reinforced by how people refer to "failed" marriages. If you internalize the societal perception, you may feel like damaged goods, and your self-esteem will suffer. In the case of false guilt, you often feel like you have failed based on someone else's expectations.

My hope is that you will be able to take ownership of any genuine guilt, work to better understand any false guilt you are carrying, seek forgiveness when appropriate, and go on to live a life of meaning and purpose.

While potential feelings of guilt, real or false, are natural depending on circumstances, you may encounter people who try to quickly explain them away. They may say things to you such as, "Don't give that a second thought. There is nothing you could have done about it. You are better off…" Whether you could actually have done something differently or not is beside the point. The point is that you are feeling as if you could have (and, if you have "real guilt, that may be very true) or should have, and you need to express these feelings to integrate them into your life. Now the key becomes finding a supportive person who won't feel a need to quickly explain away feelings of guilt, but instead allows you to explore and learn from what you are experiencing.

Other potential aspects of guilt include:

- **Relief-guilt**
  If you had a tumultuous relationship and it has now ended, you may have some relief that the relationship is finally

over. For some people, feelings of relief make them also feel guilty. "How can I feel relief after my marriage is over?" If you are feeling guilty about your relief, I urge you to find an understanding listener who can help you explore this part of your work of mourning.

- **Longstanding personality-guilt**
Some people have felt guilty their entire lives. I hope you are not one of them, but you may be. Why? Because some people learn early in life, typically during childhood, that it is their fault when something difficult happens. Experiencing a divorce is now one more thing to feel guilty about. If all-encompassing guilt is part of your experience, seek out a professional counselor who can help you work on understanding the nature and extent of your feelings.

- **Joy-guilt**
For some divorced people, after you do your work of mourning you may well begin to discover that joy reenters your life for the first time in a long time. Bravo! I'm glad for you. However, some divorced people have taught me they feel guilty about feeling joy. This is when the joy-guilt syndrome sets in. Obviously, there is no point in you desiring to be forlorn the rest of your life. As you do the work of mourning your lost relationship, your natural healing journey will allow you to start experiencing more joy and less and less pain.

If this joy-guilt phenomenon applies to you, find someone with whom you can talk it through. After all, you deserve to feel meaning and purpose in your life. Do your mourning and then move toward joy. Celebrate life and all things that delight you, that brighten your day, and make your heart glad!

If you're feeling aspects of shame, worthlessness or failure, I urge you to go backward in this book and reread divorce Misconception 2—If you get a divorce, you are a failure. This will remind you that divorce is about lost hopes and dreams, about a life with a partner who did not materialize. Yes, integrating this loss into your life is naturally challenging, but I urge you to remember you are not a failure!

Whether or not you were the one to initiate the divorce, events leading up to the divorce might leave you with feelings of rejection. Many people I have had the honor of supporting through divorce transition have found it helpful to come to the realization that the leaver is not so much rejecting the person left as much as he or she is rejecting the person he or she once was and no longer wants to be. People leave relationships for a multitude of reasons ranging from a life trauma (death of a parent sometimes sets this in motion), personal growth, changes in their life direction, or relocation. The leaver sometimes feels the only hope is to pursue a new direction in life.

If you are feeling rejected, don't try to make this journey alone. If you do, you run the risk of a massive assault on your self-esteem that may send you into a deep depression. Find a compassionate counselor or trusted friend who will help you sort through this in helpful ways.

Actually, by the time a marriage ends, each person's feelings of self-worth have often taken a nosedive. At times, self-esteem is eroded over time because of a steady stream of negative comments from your spouse. You may begin to question, "Maybe he or she is right, and I'm not a good person." Sometimes self-worth and esteem are damaged by feelings of real or false guilt, rejection, and sometimes, failure. Meddling family members may criticize, "You didn't try hard enough." Other self-appointed experts may say inappropriate things such as, "A woman's job is to never give her man a reason to

> *"It took me a long time not to judge myself through someone else's eyes."*
>
> Sally Field

stray," projecting that women are always the responsible party if a man has an affair. That is just plain ludicrous, but believe it or not, you will see some talk-show experts who espouse this philosophy.

Challenges to self-esteem sometimes come at the worst of times for divorced people—right when you are going out on your own to attempt to build a new life for yourself. Feelings of self-worth are very important to your survival when you are on this journey we are exploring together. Your self-esteem can be influenced by your capacity to seek and accept support. So, if you are struggling with self-esteem problems, do not try to go it alone. Love yourself enough to get some help. There are many things a caring counselor can do to assist you in this area. Begin right now to make your self-esteem needs a high priority and nurture yourself. You deserve it. Remember—you are going through one of life's most difficult transitions. Pay close attention to compliments that people around you give out, and take them into your heart. If there are some things you really do want to change about yourself (for example, lose weight, stop smoking, become more assertive), then get assistance to help achieve them. If you are facing the challenges of single parenting, consider taking a parenting skills course to help counter your sense of feeling overwhelmed. If you haven't already, please consider joining a divorce support group. The compassion and support usually offered up in these groups can do so much to help you with your esteem and any sense of shame, rejection or failure.

A Look Back

"I struggled so much with feeling shame about my divorce. I came from a family where the unstated rule was that you marry for life! Well, my life was not good, and my divorce freed me from living in agony. Yet, I still felt like such a failure. The best thing I did was to get in a support group and find a terrific counselor."
– a divorced woman

Self-care guidelines

If any aspect of the above dimensions (guilt, regret, self-blame, shame, rejection, worthlessness, failure) are part of our experience, seek out and find a compassionate, patient and non-judgmental listener. Whatever your feelings, acknowledge and express them openly.

As previously noted, don't allow people around you to quickly dismiss what you feel. While they may be trying to help you, this attitude will not allow you to "talk out" what you think and feel on the inside (i.e., to convert your grief into mourning). When you explore this dimension of your experience, you will come to understand the limits of your own responsibility.

As you express yourself, remember: You aren't perfect. Someone who was once your marriage partner for life no longer is. At times, you will naturally go back and review if you could have said or done anything to change where things now stand. Allow yourself this review, but as you do, be compassionate with yourself. This kind of review is often your effort to put things in perspective, to try to make sense of what you don't understand and explore missed clues about why the relationship didn't work out. (See more about this rethinking and retelling your story on p. 102.)

One of the worst things you could do is to experience some of the feelings described above, yet repress or deny them. Many physical and emotional problems will result if you try to push these feelings away without talking them out. Divorce confuses us with its timing and its disregard of our hopes, plans and dreams.

Remember—we sometimes assume that once two people commit to a relationship together, they should never come apart, so when they do, we go back and retell how what was once a "love story" has come apart. Learning to honor the mystery surrounding both the beginning and ending of your relationship is naturally difficult, yet necessary. The reality is that there are some things in life we cannot change.

Yet, there is nothing wrong with asking yourself where things went wrong. Your soul will actually benefit from an exploration of what could have been different. Just as you enter into the events and feelings at the beginning of the relationship, you have to enter into the events and feelings that come with the ending. To pull away from this natural review is to deny yourself a natural rite of passage. If the review journey feels lonely to you, do not hesitate to find a good counselor to companion you.

EXPRESS YOURSELF: Go to *The Transcending Divorce Journal*, p. 62.

Sadness, Depression, Loneliness and Vulnerability

"I just feel so sad and depressed. I have never felt this lonely before in my life. I don't know what is going to become of me," said 54-year-old Karen. "I do know I need to get some help because this is bigger than me right now. I can't concentrate, I'm not sleeping, and I'm just agitated all of the time."

Some of the most familiar aspects of divorce grief are sadness, depression, loneliness and vulnerability. Many of the things you previously counted on to provide structure, comfort and love in your life are now gone. Lost love drags us right into the middle of the wilderness.

Naturally, you don't like feeling sad, depressed, lonely or vulnerable. These experiences sap pleasure from our lives, yet these emotions that often accompany the divorce experience are so very human. Experiencing them is not a judgment about your ability to cope. You need not feel ashamed of these feelings if they apply to you. After all, they are encountered at some level by almost everyone who finds themselves in the throes of major life changes.

These emotions are often experienced in a series of rollercoaster cycles, sometimes up, sometimes down. One day may seem hopeful; the next day you are caught in an overwhelming wave of sadness. As life goes forward, you may feel incredibly vulnerable.

Someone who was once a central part of your life is now gone. Of course you feel sad, even if you were the one who initiated the end of the relationship. Of course you feel deep sorrow. Allowing yourself to feel your sadness is in large part what your journey toward healing is all about. I suggest you say out loud right now, "I have a right to feel sad!"

You also have a right to feel lonely. One person I supported noted, "Suddenly I had no one to share my meals with, my bed with, and special moments in the lives of my kids, like birthdays and holidays. I was used to having him around, and now he isn't here anymore. There is a strange emptiness in this house."

By contrast, some people who felt very lonely in the marriage are relieved to no longer be living with the other person. Yet, now there is a different

> *"Loneliness and the feeling of being unwanted is the most terrible poverty."*
> Mother Teresa

kind of loneliness to adjust to—that of literally being alone and discovering what to do with your alone time. The quiet can be a conscious reminder that now the other person is gone and your life is very different. In this vacuum, the space once occupied by the other person now creates an anxious unpredictability. Raw emotions of loss linger just below the surface, simmering and trying to surface.

Hand in hand with loneliness comes a sense of vulnerability. Vulnerability relates to the attitudes and feelings you have when confronted with the reality of lost love. It is often a time of ups and downs, a time of a multitude of emotions and disorganized, confused thinking. You may feel uncertain about yourself and your future. You have lost your way in the midst of the wilderness. You feel dazed, unable to focus. You may feel very fragile and "on edge."

Obviously I have emphasized throughout this book the theme of "being with" your feelings as this journey unfolds. If you feel this vulnerability I described above, I ask you not to think of it as "bad" and "avoidable." Divorce brings times of vulnerability. And, at a fundamental level, vulnerability is part of being human. Some things that come along in life are more powerful than we are. They leave us feeling defenseless in ways we may have never imagined. You may feel totally naked emotionally, and this feeling is not something you can simply push aside.

This is a time of many changes and instability. You are in what is called "liminal space." *Limina* is the Latin word for threshold, the space betwixt and between. Liminal space is that spiritual place we hate to be, but where the experience of divorce often takes us.

Yes, you feel because you are alive and human. Paradoxically, an effective way to cope with your vulnerability is to embrace it. In other words, honor this time of tenderness in your life. If it is helpful to you as it once was for me, think of it as a season in your life that will not last forever. Sometimes we want to rush to the next season (often from winter to spring), yet we must still endure being cold and uncomfortable for a while. You will also find guidelines for helping with your vulnerability in Touchstones Seven, Nurture Yourself, p. 133 and Touchstone Eight, Reach Out for Help, p. 159.

This time of vulnerability also requires that you set healthy boundaries in your life. Spend time with friends who support you. Don't look for a quick romance to make you feel valued and needed. Be on the alert for letting unhealthy people into your life and making poor choices that throw you off course. The things we sometimes do in an effort to short-circuit our pain usually only complicate and prolong our difficulties.

Now, allow me to return to the exploration of sadness and depression that often accompany loneliness and newfound vulnerability. Keep in mind that sometimes weeks, or even months pass before you are fully confronted by the depths of your sorrow. The slow-growing nature of this awareness is good. You could not and should not try to tolerate all of your sadness at once. Your body, mind and spirit need time to work together to embrace the depth of your loss. Be patient with yourself. Surround yourself with loving people who will understand, not judge you.

You may find that certain times and circumstances make you more sad than others. These triggers are experiences or events that reawaken past experiences. Maybe you are

"Take my word for it, the saddest thing under the sky is a soul incapable of sadness."
Madame Gasparin

driving along and "your song" comes on the radio. Maybe you see the same model of car he or she drives. Maybe you see a couple walking hand in hand as you once did. Some people find that weekends, holidays, family meals, and any kind of anniversary occasion can be hard, as can bedtime, waking up in the middle of the night, and arriving home to an empty house. Whatever your unique triggers, they often bring waves of sadness. When these waves come, you may find it helpful to reach out to a trusted friend and share the experiences, or feel your feelings and then gently move forward with your day.

Do be on alert for some people around you who might think you should be able to "control" or subdue your feelings of sadness. Nothing could be further from the truth. Your sadness is a symptom of your wound. Just as physical wounds require attention, so do emotional wounds.

Sometimes your feelings of sadness and sorrow can be overwhelming enough to be classified as clinical depression. After all, mourning that accompanies the end of a relationship can share many symptoms with depression, including sleep disturbances, appetite changes, decreased energy, withdrawal, guilt, despondency, lack of concentration, and a sense of loss of control. You may have a hard time functioning at home and at work, which may compound your feelings of isolation and helplessness.

You are probably aware that your physical body is separate from, but interconnected with, your mind and emotions. Depression can be emotional, which in turn, can upset and affect the healthy chemical balance of your body. If you stay in a depressed state for a long period of time secondary to your divorce, your body may be depleted of or begin to produce chemicals that can keep you "stuck" in your depression. When this happens, a cycle has started in which your emotional depression now involves the body as well.

What we call "biochemical depression" often has a genetic component to it that can be set in motion by non-emotional causes. When this occurs, your emotions may lapse into a depressed state. Think of it this way: If you are physically ill with the flu, you eventually feel emotionally wiped out, too. Even though things may be fine in your life while you have the flu, staying in bed for a few days can make you feel depressed. So remember, mind and body interact; they influence each other.

If you feel totally immobilized, please get help from understanding friends or better yet, a professional counselor. Help for depression sometimes involves medication, but not always. For those who do benefit from medication, helping yourself also means you must work on your emotional issues. If you're unsure if you're experiencing normal sadness or clinical depression, seek out help now (see additional information in the section titled "A Special Note About Clinical Depression and Getting Help" on the following page).

> *"Depression is the inability to construct a future."*
> Rollo May

Thoughts of suicide may occur during your divorce experience. Hundreds of divorced people have shared with me thoughts like, "I wouldn't mind if I didn't wake up tomorrow." Comments like this reflect a need to further explore the depth of your sadness. It's natural to experience these passive and passing suicidal thoughts; it is NOT natural to want to or make plans to take your own life when you go through a divorce.

If you have been thinking about taking your own life, talk to a professional helper immediately. Suicidal thoughts are sometimes an expression of wanting to find relief from the pain of your loss. Yes, you have been injured and you hurt. But to help your injury heal, you must openly acknowledge what this divorce means for you.

Self-care guidelines

As you embrace your feelings of sadness, you will need the comfort of trusted people— close friends, loving family members, and sometimes

A Look Back

"I had no energy, couldn't sleep, couldn't eat. Finally, a good friend said I needed to go get help and I did. I went to see my family physician, who got me set up with a great counselor. The counselor helped me realize I wasn't just sad, I was clinically depressed. We combined medication with counseling and I started on the path to healing. I tell everyone now: If you think you might be depressed, go get help right away." – a divorced man

A Special Note About Clinical Depression and Getting Help

For hundreds of years, most people viewed depression as a sign of physical or mental weakness, not as a real health problem. Following years of research, "clinical depression" is now recognized as a true medical disorder exacerbated by psychological and social stress. In fact, at some point in their lives, close to one-fourth of all North Americans will experience at least one episode of clinical depression.

There are a number of influences that can play a role in the development of depression, including genetics, stress (such as divorce), and change in body and brain function. Many people with clinical depression have abnormally low levels of certain brain chemicals and slowed cellular activity in areas of the brain that control mood, appetite, sleep, and other functions.

In many ways, depression and grief are similar. Common shared symptoms are feelings of sadness, lack of interest in usually pleasurable activities, and problems with eating and sleeping. The central difference is that while grief is a normal, natural, and healthy process, clinical depression is not.

These differences between grief and depression can be measured by how long the feelings last and to what extent your daily activities are impaired. Grief softens over time; clinical depression does not. After the numbing and chaotic early days and weeks of grief, your daily schedule begins to proceed as usual. If you are clinically depressed, you may be unable to function day-to-day.

Depression can complicate grief in two ways. It can create short-term symptoms that are more severe and debilitating than those normally associated with grief. In addition, clinical depression can cause symptoms of grief to persist longer than normal and potentially worsen. If you have concerns about the difference between grief and depression, seek out a trained caregiver who specializes in this area of caregiving.

I have created the following table to help both caregivers and lay people distinguish between grief and clinical depression. I suggest you review this information (placing a checkmark beside those areas that you believe apply to you).

Normal Grief	**Clinical Depression**
You have normal grief if you…	You may be clinically depressed if you…
__ respond to comfort and support.	__ do not accept support.
__ are often openly angry.	__ are irritable and complain but do not directly express anger.
__ relate your depressed feelings to the divorce experience.	__ do not relate your feelings of depression to a particular life event.
__ can still experience moments of enjoyment in life.	__ exhibit an all-pervading sense of doom.
__ exhibit feelings of sadness and emptiness.	__ project a sense of hopelessness and chronic emptiness.
__ may have transient physical complaints.	__ have chronic physical complaints.
__ express guilt over some specific aspect of the loss.	__ have generalized feelings of guilt.
__ feel a temporary loss of self-esteem.	__ feel a deep and ongoing loss of self-esteem.

Here is the great news! Depression is something that help is available for. With appropriate assessment and treatment, approximately eight out of ten people with depression will find relief from their depression. This could include you!

If you even suspect you are clinically depressed, it is critically important that you take steps to get help. Untreated depression can raise your risk for a number of additional health problems. It may also prevent you from moving forward in your divorce journey. You deserve to get help so you can continue to mourn in ways that help you heal. Choose life!

EXPRESS YOURSELF: Go to *The Transcending Divorce Journal*, p. 68.

compassionate professional helpers. Your feelings of sadness can leave you feeling isolated, alone and vulnerable.

Paradoxically, the only way to lessen your pain is to move toward it, not away from it. Moving toward your sadness is not always an easy thing to do. Sometimes when you admit to feeling sad and sorrowful, people around you may say things like, "Oh, don't be sad" or "Get a hold of yourself" or "Some people have it worse than you" or "Just think about what you have to be thankful for." Comments like these hinder, not help, you on your pathway to transcendence. If your heart and soul are preventing you from feeling your sadness, odds are your body may be harmed in the process. You have been emotionally, physically and spiritually injured. Now you must attend to your injury.

Find accepting and understanding people with whom you can express your authentic feelings. Talk to them about the divorce and what it means to you. You need people to affirm and validate what you feel. You need people who will sometimes walk with you—not behind or in front of you but beside you—on your path through the wilderness.

Keep talking until you have exhausted your capacity to talk. Doing so will help reconnect you with the world outside of yourself. Or if you can't talk it out, write it out! Paint it out! Sing it out! But get the feelings outside of yourself. And, if fitting with your personality, give yourself permission to cry—as often and as much as you need to. Tears can help cleanse your body, mind and spirit.

Consider that alone time also has some healing qualities. Spending time alone allows for reflection, introspection and development of your inner self. Over time and with work, your feelings of loneliness and emptiness can and will be replaced by inner fullness and gentle strength. You will have experienced some true personal growth when you are comfortable by yourself, no longer dependent on being around other people all the time.

Remember, I also urge you to go very slowly in terms of any new intimate relationships right now. Instead, you need to learn to be alone with yourself before you even attempt to start another love relationship. (CAVEAT: Those of you with children should also be conscious about the need to reconnect with your children before you introduce a new partner in the family dynamic.) Carefully choosing safe friends who understand your need for good boundaries right now is vitally important.

In many ways right now, you naturally feel incomplete, hurt, and confused. You desire some semblance of "normal" back in your life. In this wilderness that surrounds you, you may be vulnerable to finding someone, anyone, who will help you feel nurtured and understood. You may even be experiencing "skin hunger" and long to be touched. For some divorced people, the lack of being touched is one of the most painful parts of the journey. Yet, please remember,

"What a lovely surprise to finally discover how unlonely being alone can be."

Ellen Burstyn

you are probably vulnerable and lonely. And the reality is that one lonely, vulnerable person often unconsciously finds another lonely, vulnerable person. But this type of "connection" often has disastrous results. Protect your heart for right now; the last thing it needs is to be broken in pieces again this soon. Run, don't walk, the other way if someone who is trying to comfort you has a secondary agenda, particularly premature sexual or romantic intimacy! If you need to be touched, find a good massage therapist!

Oh, and one more point of exploration about sadness and depression. (If I sound like I'm preaching at you right now, forgive me.) Remember that temporary feelings of sadness and depression have value in your grief journey. Actually, depression is nature's way of allowing for a timeout while you heal the wounds of your grief.

Depression often slows down your body and prevents major organ systems from being damaged. Depression allows you to turn inward and slow down your spirit, too. It aids in your healing and provides time to slowly begin reordering your life. Then natural feelings can ultimately help you move ahead, to assess old ways of being, and to make plans for the future.

A caveat, however: Giving attention to, experiencing, and honoring your depressed feelings does not mean staying stuck in them for years and years. Nor does it mean using depression as an excuse to remain a victim or to get struck in resentment and bitterness. Do your work of mourning, renew your divine spark, live your life deeply and fully, not only healing yourself, but eventually reaching out and re-engaging in the world around you!

EXPRESS YOURSELF: Go to *The Transcending Divorce Journal*, p. 65.

Relief, Release, Happiness, Euphoria and Hope

Thirty-year-old Bob said, "I am free of living in the midst of a battleground. We had very few normal, relaxed conversations in our marriage of eight years. I didn't feel like I could do anything right. Now I feel tremendous relief and hope for a new life."

Sometimes you may feel aspects of relief and release when you get a divorce. Some people even use the words happiness and euphoria to describe their experiences. If your relationship was full of conflict, you had irreconcilable differences, or something dramatic happened to push you apart, you may well be one of those people who feel relief when the marriage is over.

Maybe you feel like your relationship ended long before you divorced. Some people mourn the end of their marriage

"Many divorces are not really the result of irreparable injury but involve, instead, a desire on the part of the man or woman to shatter the setup, start out from scratch alone, and make life work for them all over again. They want the risk of disaster, want to touch bottom, see where bottom is, and, coming up, to breathe the air with relief and relish again."

Edward Hoagland

long before it actually ends. Now, you may just be glad it is finally over.

Also, if you get a divorce from someone who abused you, you may feel a tremendous sense of relief that equates with a feeling of being safe for the first time in a long time. This is natural and appropriate.

Another form of relief comes for some people when they give expression to long-repressed thoughts and feelings surrounding the circumstances of the divorce. If you have repressed or denied these feelings before, when you do express them, you may feel as if a great pressure has been lifted from your head, heart and soul.

Do be alert to the reality that you may have some initial relief when your divorce is final, but you may also have some rollercoaster emotions in the weeks and months ahead. Some people are sailing along and then get shocked when waves of loss and sadness set in down the line. If this happens to you, remember there is nothing wrong with you. Instead, you are discovering that mourning the loss of a relationship is experienced in a wave-like fashion. Sometimes happy, even euphoric periods come between periods of confusion and explosive emotions. As you make movement, or perturbate, you will eventually become more competent in your new phase of life and be less vulnerable to these emotional ups and downs. Oh, and enjoy your life-affirming happiness when it comes your way, because you can and will eventually experience it! In part, that is what this book is all about.

A Look Back

"It was not a good marriage from the get go. He was selfish and self-absorbed. Everything was all about his needs. He patronized me and didn't even know he was doing it. I married him because of some unhealthy family-of-origin issues. I got some good counseling, had tons of valuable insights and got the heck out of the marriage. I've never been more relieved in my life." – a divorced woman

When appropriate, allowing yourself to acknowledge relief as a part of your divorce experience can be a critical step in your journey through divorce grief. Yes, the divorce experience can sometimes be overwhelming and painful and, at the same time, relieving and hopeful. Whatever your feelings, working to embrace them creates the opportunity to find hope in your healing.

Self-care guidelines

There may be some very good reasons you feel relief, release, happiness, euphoria, or hope. If you do, find someone who will not judge you while you voice this dimension of your experience. If you don't want to talk about it, use the companion journal and write about it.

EXPRESS YOURSELF: Go to *The Transcending Divorce Journal*, p. 68.

A Final Thought About the Feelings You May Experience

As you journey through the wilderness of your grief, over time and with the support of others, you will come to experience what I like to describe as "integration." When you come out on the other side of the wilderness and you are able to fully enjoy life and living again, you have encountered the integration of your divorce transition. You will learn more about this important concept in Touchstone Nine. But before we get there, let's explore some of the other trail markers to watch for on your path to healing.

Touchstone Five

Recognize You Are Not Crazy

"If you are sure you understand everything that is going on, you are hopelessly confused."

Walter Mondale

Divorce invariably brings major changes in the circumstances of everyday living, and people often wonder if they are "going crazy." The two most common questions I get as a counselor to people experiencing divorce are, in fact, "Am I crazy?" and "Am I normal?" Be assured that most people experience thoughts, feelings, and experiences that seem out of the ordinary and make little sense during this time of major transition. Hundreds of people have said to me, "I just don't feel like myself."

The journey through divorce can be so radically different from our everyday realities that sometimes it feels more like being picked up and dropped onto the surface of the moon than it does a trek through the wilderness. The terrain is so completely foreign and disorienting, and our behaviors in that terrain seem so out of whack, that we feel like we are going crazy.

As one man reflected, "When I was going through my divorce I felt like I was going crazy. I was on an emotional rollercoaster and I couldn't seem to get off. One day I would seem okay, and the next day I wasn't sure I could get my feet out of bed. I couldn't keep track of time, felt more helpless than anytime in my life, and kept going into the bathroom to cry my eyes out."

This man wasn't crazy, and you're not either. You may be experiencing thoughts and feelings that seem crazy because they are so unusual to you. Actually, what is unusual in life is often usual in grief—and, as you have learned, divorce creates grief and the need to mourn.

This Touchstone helps you to be on the lookout for the trail marker that affirms your sanity: Recognize you are not crazy. It's an important trail marker, because if you miss it, your entire journey through the wilderness of your grief may feel like Alice's surreal visit to Wonderland. Actually your journey may still feel surreal, even if you find this trail marker, but at least you'll know in your head, and, I hope, your heart, that you're not going crazy.

Following are a number of potential experiences that cause us divorced people to feel like we might be going crazy. They may or may not be a part of your personal experience. My intent is not to prescribe what should be happening to you. Instead, I encourage you to become familiar with what you may encounter while in the wilderness of your divorce experience. Remember to use your companion journal to explore how each of the following experiences might apply to you.

Sudden Changes in Mood

The divorce journey can make you feel like you are surviving fairly well one minute and in the depths of despair the next. Sudden changes in your mood are a difficult, yet natural, part of your experience. You are on an "emotional rollercoaster." These mood changes can be small or dramatic. They can be triggered by driving past a familiar place, the lyrics of a song, an insensitive comment made by someone, or even a change in the weather.

Mood changes can make you feel like you are going crazy because your inappropriate self-expectations may be that you should follow a pattern of continued motion forward. In other words, you may expect yourself to keep feeling better and better.

In reality, your emotions twist and turn like a mountainous trail. One minute you might be feeling great and the next, lousy.

Sometimes, those who leave or initially file for the divorce feel an initial sense of relief, yet six to eighteen months later, experiences large waves of emotion (including sadness) that pull their feet out from under them. Yet for others who are "leavers," this wave never comes. The key is to face whatever comes, feel your feelings and integrate them into your being.

> *"The art of living does not consist in preserving and clinging to a particular mood of happiness, but in allowing happiness to change its form without being disappointed by the change, for happiness, like a child, must be allowed to grow up."*
>
> Charles Morgan

If you have these ups and downs, don't be hard on yourself. Instead, have patience and be patient with yourself. As you allow yourself to mourn your lost relationship and move toward healing, the periods of hopelessness will be replaced by periods of hopefulness.

EXPRESS YOURSELF: Go to *The Transcending Divorce Journal*, p. 72.

Leftover or Residual Attachment

Many divorced people experience aspects of lingering attachment to the spouse they divorced. Uncertainty, mixed feelings and conflicting emotions often reflect this phenomenon. These leftover feelings of connection reflect that attachment can go on longer than genuine love does. They also occur in many people despite a history of ongoing antagonism and conflict.

Socialist Robert Weiss was among the first people to write about and research this experience. He found that this lingering sense of attachment is somewhat more common among those who are left and somewhat more common in men than in women.

This lingering emotional attachment reflects the history of bonding that took place. It is not always so easy, even when there is good reason for a relationship to end, to simply make a clean break. The world feels different and, at times, less safe, without this person who was an important person in your life. This residual attachment can sometimes paralyze a person with fear in ways that "hold" him or her in the relationship. Some people even fight all settlement agreements in an effort to delay the divorce from being finalized.

For some people, this experience prevents them from getting on with life and developing a new self-identity. There are times when close proximity or shared custody of children makes this experience even more naturally complicated. This leftover attachment contributes to the emotional rollercoaster for many people.

> *"When two people decide to get a divorce, it isn't a sign that they 'don't understand' one another, but a sign that they have, at last, begun to."*
>
> Helen Rowland

If you feel a lingering need for attachment, you may have a difficult time for a while, but it may be somewhat easier if you know that this experience is not uncommon. You may vacillate between longing for your ex and wanting to push him or her away once and for all. You may question, "Am I doing the right thing to get a divorce or is this the biggest mistake of my life?"

EXPRESS YOURSELF: Go to *The Transcending Divorce Journal*, p. 72.

Rethinking and Retelling the Story

Often when a relationship ends, you find yourself with a need to think and talk about your marriage and the circumstances of the divorce over and over again. You may go through the same events in your mind repeatedly. You may feel like you can't "shake" your memories of certain moments: what each partner did and said; what each partner could have done differently; where things went wrong; the fights; who is to blame; good times and bad. You may replay these memories over and over in your mind and question your sanity.

You may also feel the need—almost a compulsion—to tell other people about these prominent memories again and again. You may find yourself wanting to talk about them all the time. Essentially, you are constructing your account of what was once a love story but has now become a divorce story.

I call this natural process "storying." Telling the story isn't a sign that you are crazy; in fact, it's a sign that you're doing your work of mourning this major life change. Whether

> *"All human beings have an innate need to hear and tell stories and to have a story to live by."*
> Harvey Cox

you're conscious of this fact or not, you tell yourself the story in an effort to integrate it into your life. Each time you go through the events of your marriage, the onset of problems, and your divorce, more of the pieces fall into place.

Essentially, what has happened to you is so hard to fathom that your mind compels you to revisit it again and again until you've truly acknowledged it and embraced its reality. Telling the story brings what you know in your head and what you feel in your heart together.

Allow yourself this necessary review. Don't be angry with yourself if you can't seem to stop repeating your story, whether in your mind or aloud to others. The telling of your story is an inherent need as you wander through the wilderness. Watch out for people who don't understand this phenomenon and say hurtful things like, "Obsessing over it won't change anything," or "You need to put the past in the past and get on with your life." Blocking your need to tell the story won't help you on your path to healing and transcendence.

Yes, it hurts to constantly think about your relationship, partner, life as a married person and the divorce. But remember—usually grief wounds require going backward before you can go forward. Be compassionate with yourself. Try to surround yourself with people who allow and encourage you to repeat whatever you need to repeat. Support groups are helpful to many people because there is a mutual understanding of the need to "tell the story." I strongly believe that when you allow yourself to story, grace happens!

EXPRESS YOURSELF: Go to *The Transcending Divorce Journal*, p. 73.

Time Distortion

"I don't know what day it is, let alone what time it is!" This kind of comment is not unusual when you are going through a divorce. Sometimes, time moves so quickly; at other times, it crawls. Your sense of past and future also may seem to be frozen in place. You may lose track of what day, month, or even year it is. Your inability to keep time right now isn't crazy. Actually, it is common, particularly in the early days and weeks of a separation or divorce.

EXPRESS YOURSELF: Go to *The Transcending Divorce Journal*, p. 73.

Self-Focus

Especially early in your divorce experience, you may find yourself being less conscious of the needs of others. You may not want to listen to other people's problems. You may not have the energy to attend to all of the needs of your children or other family members. You may feel flustered or disheartened that the world is still turning while your life is at a complete standstill.

The reality that during this experience you are less tuned in to the needs of others and are instead focusing on your own thoughts and feelings doesn't mean you're crazy or selfish. What is does mean is that you have an emotional need that is calling you to give more of your attention and energy to yourself right now. Your mind and spirit are directing your attention away from others and into yourself because you need to do this in order to integrate your grief and discover a new identity. Don't feel guilty or shame yourself for these feelings. They are a necessary part of your grief work.

Later on you'll be ready to reconnect with others and support them in their life trials. If you need help caring for dependent children, try to find some caring friends and family who can assist you for a while. Of course, your children's needs are very important, but it is okay to acknowledge that there are times when you are unable to be as available to them as you'd like and need to call in reinforcements.

"Self-pity in its early stages is as snug as a feather mattress. Only when it hardens does it become uncomfortable."

Maya Angelou

Some people may attempt to take your grief away from you by trying to keep you from any kind of self-focus. They may want you to quickly reenter the "regular" world because they don't understand your need for a temporary retreat. If turning inward is part of your experience, be assured you are normal.

When you are in pain before, during and after divorce, the turning inward and the need for self-focus is analogous to what occurs when you have a physical wound. You cover a physical wound with a bandage for a period of time. Then you expose the wound to the open air, which helps with healing but also risks contamination. The emotional, physical and spiritual pain that accompanies divorce certainly demands the same kind of protection.

The word *temporary* is important here, however. You may move back and forth between needing time alone and needing time with other people. If you stay in a self-focused, inward mode, you may risk developing a pattern of not expressing how your divorce transition is impacting you. As you well know by now, not expressing yourself and exploring how your life is reshaped by this experience will stunt your healing process.

EXPRESS YOURSELF: Go to *The Transcending Divorce Journal*, p. 74.

Powerlessness and Helplessness

Your encounter with divorce can sometimes leave you feeling powerless. You may think or say, "What am I going to do? I feel so completely helpless." Perhaps you would like to be able to "re-do" some elements of your relationship by traveling back in time to the beginning of your relationship but you can't. You may wish there were things you could have changed about the relationship or your partner, but feel powerless in the knowledge that you can't.

Also, you may wonder what could have been if only some things were different. Could the divorce have been prevented? Could you have tried harder to make it work? These "if onlys" and "what ifs" are often expressions of wishing you could have had more control

"Please be kind and compassionate, O Lord of my life; I am helpless, and I seek Your Sanctuary, God. Please, give me Your Hand, and lift me up, out of the deep dark pit."
Atharva Veda

over something you could not, be it your spouse's behavior or your own. Lack of control of aspects of a relationship or person that you once cared deeply about is a difficult reality to accept. Still, it is one that, over time and through the work of mourning, you will and you must allow yourself to encounter. These feelings of helplessness and powerlessness in the face of this painful reality are normal and natural.

Almost paradoxically, by acknowledging and allowing for temporary feelings of helplessness, you help yourself. When you try to "stay strong," you often get yourself into trouble. Share your feelings with people you trust and who are capable of being compassionate companions to you. Remember—expressed divorce grief is diminished divorce grief; find someone to talk to who will listen without sitting in judgment of your thoughts and feelings or the ways you express these outwardly.

EXPRESS YOURSELF: Go to *The Transcending Divorce Journal*, p. 74.

Griefbursts and Triggers

As one woman said, "I was just going through my day, and then this song, which used to be our song, came on the radio, and I had these overwhelming feelings of sadness and I felt my heart literally ache." As I mentioned in Touchstone Two, I call this a "griefburst," which is a sudden, sharp feeling of grief that can result in anxiety, sadness, and pain. Some people call it a grief attack, because they seem to attack you without warning.

Some people think that long periods of deep sadness make up the bulk of the typical divorce journey. Actually, you may more frequently encounter acute and episodic "pangs" or "spasms" of grief between some less painful blocks of time. What triggers a spasm are the events, often tied to sensory modes (seeing something, hearing something, smelling something) that reawaken past experiences and result in griefbursts.

During a griefburst, you may feel an overwhelming sense of missing aspects of what once was and find yourself openly crying, or perhaps even sobbing. One man told me, "I was at the store the other day and looked up and saw the spaghetti—she made the best spaghetti—and that was all it took. I started crying like a baby right there on aisle six of the grocery store."

Griefbursts may feel like "crazy bursts," but they are a normal and necessary part of the divorce experience. When and if one strikes you, be compassionate with yourself. You have every right to feel temporary paralysis or loss of control. Whatever you do, don't try to deny a griefburst when it comes to surface. It is probably more powerful than you are. Call a friend to share the experience. Don't be ashamed of your human vulnerability. You invested a lot in a relationship, and now you are genuinely touched by triggers that remind you of what once was.

EXPRESS YOURSELF: Go to *The Transcending Divorce Journal*, p. 75.

Crying and Sobbing

If you're crying and sobbing a lot, you may feel like you never will stop, which can trigger your feelings of going crazy. Sobbing is like wailing, and it comes from the inner core of your being. Sobbing is an expression of the deep, strong emotions within you. These emotions need to get out, and sobbing allows for their release.

In many Eastern cultures, sobbing and wailing (sometimes called *keening*) are encouraged and understood as a normal part of grief and mourning life's losses. In our culture, however, sobbing is often considered strange and feels frightening to observers. It is perceived as being "out of control" or "dramatic." (This misconception that many other people have is likely where your feelings of loss of control come from!) The reality is you do not have control of this situation, and it is this very loss of control that helps you express your strong feelings. Your feelings are too strong to be "under control" inside you – and their authentic expression can't be under control either.

> *"Weeping is perhaps the most human and universal of relief measures."*
> Karl Menninger

If you're crying or sobbing a lot, you're not crazy. Cry, wail, and sob as long and as hard and as often as you need to. Don't try to be strong and brave for yourself or anyone else. Tears have a voice of their own. You will be wise to allow yours to speak to you. Let your tears speak, listen to the tears and heal.

EXPRESS YOURSELF: Go to *The Transcending Divorce Journal*, p. 75.

Borrowed Tears

Here's another kind of crying that can make you feel like you're going crazy—borrowed tears. Borrowed tears are tears that spring up when you are touched by something you see, hear, or smell. During a griefburst, you might be brought to tears by a place or a smell that directly reminds you of your former love.

Borrowed tears, on the other hand, seem to come out of nowhere and are triggered by something you don't associate with your ex-spouse and wouldn't normally have been upset by.

Borrowed tears are called what they are called because you seem to be "borrowing" them from someone else's store of pain and memory. They're not yours! You might find yourself crying at a sappy commercial on TV or seeing a little bird out your window. These things never made you sad before. Why are you crying now?

You're crying because your heart and soul are hurting and your emotions are tender. Think of it this way: If you press on your leg gently with your hand, it doesn't hurt. But if you break your leg and then press on it, even the slightest touch can hurt. Your heart is broken now, and anything that touches your heart even slightly may hurt. This is normal and will pass as your heart continues to heal.

EXPRESS YOURSELF: Go to *The Transcending Divorce Journal*, p. 76.

Painful Linking Objects and Memorabilia

Linking objects and memorabilia are items that you have around that remind you of your relationship and the person you are divorced from. These include belongings such as photographs, wedding rings, gifts, books, clothing and other formally prized connections to your relationship. Seeing these things can naturally trigger all sorts of feelings, ranging from sadness to resentment to intense anger. When this happens, you may feel a little out of control, or "crazy." Again, remember, you are not crazy, you are human and you are allowing yourself to feel.

Early on in your break-up, you may need to box some of these items up and store them away for a while. Whatever you do, don't impulsively throw them all away. As time passes and you do your work of mourning the lost relationship, it can actually be helpful to go through these linking objects. While there is no specific timeframe for doing this, trust your instincts about taking each item out one by one and reflecting on the memories, both good and bad, connected to them. Allow yourself to mourn as you embrace these memories.

Eventually, you will probably discover that this memorabilia has less control over you and that you can make realistic decisions about what to do with it. There may be a few things you want to keep; however, as part of your need to disengage from your spouse and complete your emotional divorce, you will probably need to get rid of many of the linking objects that keep you connected. If you are confused or feel immobilized by what to do with those items, find a good counselor to help you with this naturally difficult process.

EXPRESS YOURSELF: Go to *The Transcending Divorce Journal*, p. 76.

Carried Grief From Prior Losses

Some of the pain you might encounter in your divorce experience can potentially come from what I call "carried grief" from prior losses. Some people, through no fault of their own, carry longstanding and cumulative grief, often stemming from their childhood.

If this is part of your experience, you are at risk now of additional suffering because of these unacknowledged and unexpressed feelings of loss. You may have many ghosts of grief—that is, many unacknowledged losses—or you may find that your ghost is identifiably singular—a specific loss that devastated you, even if you didn't realize it at the time.

Now, as you experience the loss of your present relationship, you may have some symptoms (such as generalized anxiety, panic attacks, depression) that are invitations to go backward and give attention to your prior losses that were never fully mourned and integrated into your life. Sometimes you cannot mourn current losses and life transitions until you go backward and work on your previous carried griefs.

Experience has taught me that some people feel crazy because of this phenomenon of carried grief. The good news is that if this does apply to you, there are ways of getting help to do catch-up mourning. If you want to learn more about this and make a plan to help yourself, see my book *Living in the Shadow of the Ghosts of Grief: Step Into the Light.*

"There is no grief like the grief that does not speak."

Henry Wadsworth Longfellow

EXPRESS YOURSELF: Go to *The Transcending Divorce Journal*, p. 77.

Suicidal Thoughts

We touched on suicidal thoughts in Touchstone Four, but this subject is important enough to reemphasize here. Thoughts that come and go about questioning if you want to go on living can be a normal part of your grief and mourning. You might say or think, "It'd be so much easier not to be here" or "I can't bear to see what we've built fall apart." Usually this thought is not so much an active wish to kill yourself as it is a wish to avoid or ease your pain.

To have these thoughts is normal and not crazy; however, to make plans and take action to end your life is extremely concerning and not a normal response to divorce. Sometimes your body, mind, and spirit can hurt so much that you wonder if you will ever feel alive again. Just remember that in doing the hard work of mourning your divorce, you can and will find continued meaning in life. Let yourself be helped as you discover hope for your healing.

If thoughts of suicide take on planning and structure, make certain that you get help immediately. Sometimes tunnel vision can prevent you from seeing choices. You have the capacity to mourn this major life change and go on to rediscover a life filled with meaning and purpose.

EXPRESS YOURSELF: Go to *The Transcending Divorce Journal*, p. 77.

Medicating Your Feelings With Alcohol and Drugs

As emphasized throughout this book, feelings will be integrated into your life only as they are expressed. Unfortunately, when you experience divorce, you may be tempted to want to quickly quell your feelings of grief. Many people who would not usually be vulnerable to abusing alcohol and drugs fall into this trap when a relationship has ended. But inappropriate and indiscriminate use of alcohol and drugs to avoid pain only brings temporary relief from a hurt that must ultimately be embraced. (The use of prescription drugs when appropriately prescribed and monitored is different than what I'm exploring with you here.)

While some people try to self-treat their wounded soul with substances, others will use excessive behaviors to numb their sorrow. Examples might include: excess eating; premature replacement of the relationship (which often includes hyper-sexuality); excess working; excess busyness; excess shopping (better known as "retail" therapy); excess exercise; excess caring for everyone else to the exclusion of self; excess risk-taking (such as gambling or driving under the influence of chemicals); excess traveling; and excess nicotine (after a divorce, some people start smoking, while existing smokers often increase this behavior—and yes, nicotine is a drug!).

Yes, there are numerous ways to try to go *around* grief instead of *through* it. Many of these can make you feel like you are going "crazy." However, despite attempts to numb, deny, or go around divorce loss, your wounded soul still needs to be given the attention it deserves.

One additional caveat here: Some people are predisposed to problems in this area because they tend to have what we call an "addictive personality." These people tend to over-engage with things they become involved with. This is where one drink leads to many more drinks; a little spending leads to a lot of spending; a little work leads to overwork; a little helping out others leads to codependent caretaking. You can probably discern if this description applies to you. If so, be aware of it and be on guard related to this tendency. What may on the surface seem like a form of temporary relief may result in huge additional chaos in your life. And, if you reflect on this reality, you probably already have more than enough chaos going on surrounding your divorce transition. Don't make yourself feel even crazier with these kinds of self-treating behaviors.

EXPRESS YOURSELF: Go to *The Transcending Divorce Journal*, p. 78.

Dreams and Nightmares

Sometimes, the process of disengaging from your spouse physically will be far easier than getting him or her out of your head. Dreaming a lot about your former spouse may contribute to your feelings of going crazy. Some people cannot stop thinking about their former spouse, even in their sleep!

Keep in mind that dreams are one of the ways some people do aspects of the work of mourning. They can be part of that natural evade and encounter process explored in Touchstone Four. You may dream of being back together and then separating again. You may be trying to help yourself "move on" through replaying the end of the relationship in your dreams. You may dream of being intimate with this person again.

The content of your dreams often reflects changes in your grief journey. You may have one kind of dream early in your divorce experience and another later on. Often you are trying to dislodge your former partner from your life and acknowledge your new reality. Actually, part of acknowledging your new reality is challenging yourself about any lingering, false hopes for reconnection to your partner, and dreams can help you do this. If you are dreaming about your relationship or your ex-spouse, you are not crazy.

So if dreams are part of your trek through the wilderness, make use of them to better understand where you have been, where you are, and where you are going. Also, find a skilled listener who won't interpret your dreams to you, but who will help you discover what your dreams mean to you!

On the other hand, some people experience nightmares, particularly if there has been a history of abuse or extensive trauma surrounding the divorce.

"Those with the greatest awareness have the greatest nightmares."

Mahatma Gandhi

These experiences can be very frightening. If you are having nightmares, talk about them with someone who can support and understand you.

EXPRESS YOURSELF: Go to *The Transcending Divorce Journal*, p. 79.

Anniversary and Holiday Occasions

Naturally, anniversary and holiday occasions can bring back memories of precious times, some happy, some sad. Birthdays (your ex's and your own), your wedding date, family-oriented holidays like Easter, Thanksgiving, Hanukkah, and Christmas, invite you to reflect and think of what you did together on these occasions.

Early on in your divorce journey, you may experience griefbursts during some of these times. On the other hand, if these events were always times of turmoil, you may find that you feel more joyful or peaceful during these occasions. You may actually discover a newfound enthusiasm for the holidays.

"You can clutch the past so tightly to your chest that it leaves your arms too full to embrace the present."

Jan Glidewell

If you're having a really tough time on special days, you're not crazy. Plan ahead and remember that few holidays go perfectly, whether you are happily married or without a partner. If you are struggling, do not suffer in silence. Recognize you need support and map out how to get it. Also, the really good news is that these special days do get easier as you do your mourning and gently and self-compassionately move forward with your life.

EXPRESS YOURSELF: Go to *The Transcending Divorce Journal*, p. 80.

You're Not Crazy, You're Transitioning

Never forget that your journey through the wilderness of divorce may bring you through all kinds of strange and unfamiliar terrain. As I said at the beginning of this chapter, your experiences may seem so alien that you feel more like you're on the moon! When it seems like you are going crazy, remind yourself to look for this trail marker that assures you that you're *not* going crazy. You are experiencing a major life transition that requires that you confront many new changes and challenges. Don't judge yourself; instead be self-loving and patient, and seek compassionate support from people around you. And remember, you will eventually get where you need to go.

Touchstone Six

Understand the Six Needs of Divorce Transition

If you are hoping for a map for your journey through the experience of divorce, none exists. *Your* wilderness is an undiscovered wilderness and you are its first explorer.

But those of us who have experienced divorce have found that our paths have many similarities. In fact, there are more commonalities than there are differences. In an effort to describe these similarities, a number of authors have proposed models of grief that refer to "stages." (For example, one such model describes three stages: shock, adjustment, and growth.) But, as we observed in Touchstone Two about grief misconceptions, we do not go through orderly and predictable stages of divorce with clear-cut beginnings and endings.

But when we experience divorce transition, we do have some similar needs. Instead of referring to stages, I have found that we go through six central needs of divorce transition. As I said in the Introduction, as we journey through divorce, we need to follow the trail markers, or the Touchstones, if we are to find our way out of the wilderness. The trail marker we will discuss in this chapter reminds us that there are six central needs of mourning during divorce transition. You might think of Touchstone Six as its own little grouping of trail markers.

You will find that several of the six needs I will explore with you reiterate and reinforce concepts found in other chapters of this book. I hope this reinforcement helps you embrace how very important these fundamental concepts are.

Keep in mind that, unlike the stages of divorce you might have heard about, the six needs outlined below are not orderly, predictable or linear. You will probably jump around in random fashion while working on them. You will address each need when you are ready to do so. Sometimes you will be working on more than one need at a time. Your awareness of these needs, however, will allow you to be an active participant in integrating this transition into your life as opposed to perceiving this life transition as something you passively experience.

The Six Needs of Divorce Transition

1. Acknowledge the reality of the divorce.

2. Let yourself feel the pain of the divorce.

3. Shift your relationship with your former spouse.

4. Develop a new self-identity.

5. Search for meaning.

6. Let others help you—now and always.

Need 1: Acknowledge the Reality of the Divorce

You can know something in your head but not in your heart. Your emotional divorce is not the same as your legal divorce, and these often do not unfold at the same time or pace. This first need is a close cousin to Touchstone One (open to the presence of your loss), which involves confronting the reality of the end of your marriage. For some people, this necessary step doesn't take place until long after the legal divorce.

Whether the divorce was sudden and traumatic, or gradual and anticipated, acknowledging the full reality of the divorce may occur over weeks and months. You may feel like you are in a bad dream and keep hoping you will wake up and your ex will walk through the door. To survive, you may try to push away the reality of the divorce at times. Embracing your new reality is usually not quick, easy or efficient. Yet, it must be done so you can eventually move forward with your new life, free of the ties that bind you. For your own benefit, you won't want to see this as an elusive goal, but as an achievable goal. Otherwise, you will be at risk for merely existing, not truly living.

As you encounter this process, you may move back and forth between protesting and encountering the reality of your divorce. You may discover yourself replaying events surrounding the divorce and confronting memories, both good and bad. What went wrong? What led to the divorce? Constructing your account of the divorce, or "storying," is an inherent part of this need. It's as if each time you review it, the divorce becomes a little more real. Very gradually, by going backward and "telling the story," most people begin to go forward. Some people never do befriend this need, but I don't want you to be among them.

"Wounds cannot heal as long as they are denied."
Alice Miller

You will want to actively participate in the dance surrounding this need. One moment the reality of the divorce may be unbearable; another moment it may be welcomed. At yet another moment, it may feel tolerable. Be patient with this need while at the same time creating some momentum to keep "dosing" yourself with your new reality. As you express what you think and feel outside of yourself in doses, you will be working on this important need.

Telling people that you are divorcing or are divorced is a part of this need. Making other people aware of your divorce helps you begin to start feeling like a single person instead of a married one. Also, telling people about your divorce serves as a rite of passage that marks the end of your marriage and the beginning of your life as a single person. Letting people know about your new single status also activates some support when you need it the very most.

Remember that this first need of mourning, like the other five that follow, may intermittently require your attention for months. Be patient and compassionate with yourself as you work on each need.

EXPRESS YOURSELF: Go to *The Transcending Divorce Journal*, p. 84.

Need 2: Let Yourself Feel the Pain of the Divorce

Like Touchstone One (open to the presence of your loss), this need of mourning requires us to embrace the pain of our divorce experience—something we naturally don't want to do. It is easier to avoid, repress or deny the pain that accompanies this major life transition, yet it is in confronting our pain that we learn to reconcile ourselves to it. Whether you were the leaver or the left, pain is part of your journey. The symptoms explored in Touchstone Four (shock, disorganization, explosive emotions, etc.) are reflections of the reality of your pain.

You will probably discover that you need to dose yourself in embracing your painful symptoms that come with the journey. In other words, you cannot (nor should you try to) overload yourself with hurt all the time. Sometimes you may need to distract yourself or take a time-out from the pain of the divorce, while at other times you will need to create a safe place to move toward it.

Feeling your pain can sometimes zap you of energy. When your energy is low, you may be tempted to suppress your feelings of hurt and loss or even run from them. If you start running and keep running, you may never heal. Yes, you must allow yourself to feel your pain in doses.

Unfortunately, as I have said, our culture tends to encourage the denial of pain surrounding life losses, including divorce. We misunderstand the role of hurt, pain, even suffering. If you openly express feelings of grief, misinformed friends may advise you to "carry on" or "keep your chin up" or, worse yet, tell you that "you are better off without him or her." If, on the other hand, you remain "strong" and "in control," you may be congratulated for "doing well" with your divorce. Actually, in many ways "doing well" with your divorce also means befriending the pain that reflects your special needs right now. Don't let others deny you this critical need of divorce transition.

"We must embrace pain and burn it as fuel for our journey."
Kenji Miyazawa

If you are a man, be aware that this need may be particularly difficult to meet. You may be conditioned to deny pain and encouraged to keep your feelings inside. You may expect yourself to be strong and in control. Yet, despite your efforts at self-control, you may now be experiencing a variety of feelings at an intensity level you never thought possible. To slow down, turn inward and embrace hurt may be foreign to you. I hope you have caring friends who will be understanding, patient and tolerant with you.

As you encounter your pain, you will also need to continue to nurture yourself physically, emotionally, cognitively, socially, and spiritually. Eat well, rest often, and exercise regularly. Find others with whom you can share your painful thoughts and feelings; friends who listen without judging are your most important helpers as you work on this important need. Of course, a sensitive counselor to companion you can also be an invaluable resource,

Never forget that you are engaged in a naturally difficult, rocky life transition *process*, not an easy, smooth, life-transition *event*. Your pain will probably ebb and flow for quite some time; embracing it when it washes over you will require patience, support, and courage.

EXPRESS YOURSELF: Go to *The Transcending Divorce Journal*, p. 85.

Need 3: Shift Your Relationship With Your Former Spouse

This need of divorce transition involves disengaging from your prior relationship with your former life partner. Shifting your relationship is a vital step in completing your emotional divorce. While not always easy, particularly when children are involved, it is a necessary step in moving toward your new and different life.

My hope is that you don't misunderstand this need. To shift your relationship does not mean that you have to permanently end your relationship with your ex-spouse. Obviously, if you have children, to completely end your relationship should not even be a consideration. The ability to communicate respectfully with your ex about the children and their needs will be helpful to both of you, and most important, your children.

"We owned what we learned back there; the experience and the growth are grafted into our lives."

Ellen Goodman

However, to evolve into an effective relationship in the future, your relationship will need to be restructured and redefined. As hard as it might be, you will have to *stop* interacting in old ways and work to create mutually acceptable new ways of communicating. In addition, because of the naturally intense emotion that accompanies the initial break up, a period of little or no involvement (a time out) may be required prior to a newly defined relationship taking place in a way that will work. Of course, if you don't have children, you do have the option of permanently ending the relationship as opposed to redefining and restructuring it.

While all of the following actions may or may not help you in your unique situation, some can probably be of help in shifting or redefining your relationship:

• *Establish clear boundaries in your relationship.* For example, limit your contact with each other to required issues only, such as children. If you don't have children, avoid coming up with reasons to see or talk to each other.

- *If you must communicate, formalize how you will communicate*; set pre-arranged, time-limited meetings or phone calls.

- *Do not involve each other in any of the functions (with the exception of parenting) that she or he had responsibility for in the marriage* (laundry, bill paying, car maintenance). You want to stay out of your old relationship and build a new life for yourself.

- *If you have children, formalize new parenting responsibilities*. Arrange a schedule that details when the children will be with each of you. This prearranged schedule will help eliminate the need for constant communication to arrange movement of the children back and forth. Once the schedule is set, stick with it! An additional benefit of the set schedule is that it will limit inappropriate power plays surrounding the children.

- *Respect the privacy of your former spouse*. Do not offer up personal information and do not ask any of him or her. Remember: You are creating new boundaries.

- *If you have children, learn to co-parent effectively*. While the principles of co-parenting are beyond the scope of this book, I can tell you that this concept is crucial to your children's future well-being. I encourage you to read books, attend classes and perhaps see a counselor who can help with this.

- *Openly acknowledge your divorce*. Telling people helps you shift the relationship and reminds you that you have started a new and changed life.

- *Allow yourself to mourn the end of your relationship* and all of the secondary losses (see p. 24) that come with it.

- *Consider acknowledging the shift in your relationship with a divorce ritual or ceremony*. There are a number of resources available that can help you plan and carry out this kind of experience. This rite of passage will often help you (and your children) with the shift in the relationship.

- *If distorted anger directed at your former spouse has put you on hold, consider taking back control of your life through forgiveness*. Uncontrolled anger sometimes prevents you from shifting from the old relationship to the new relationship. Continuing to replay past injuries or trying to seek revenge will keep you tied to the past, not hoping for and building your new future. Remember, if circumstances are such that you need to forgive, you are by no means saying that any wrongdoing was justified. Usually, forgiveness isn't something you are doing for your former spouse, it is something you are doing to free you to go on with your life and take back control.

Again, these are only a few general guidelines to assist you in restructuring, redefining and shifting your relationship with your former spouse. As you reflect on this need and have any insights that this is a real struggle for you, please consider seeking professional counseling to assist you. Your future will become open to a new life to the extent that you shift from the old life.

EXPRESS YOURSELF: Go to *The Transcending Divorce Journal*, p. 86.

Need 4: Develop a New Self-Identity

Your personal identity, or self-perception, is the result of the ongoing developmental process of establishing an awareness of who you are. Part of your self-identity comes from the relationships you have with other people. When you go through a divorce, your self-identity, or the way you see yourself, changes.

As a married person, you defined yourself as a couple, as a team. When you joined together as a couple, you tried to develop a way of living together that worked for the two of you. New roles and behaviors evolved over time as you created your team identity. In your marriage you were a "wife" or a "husband" with specific roles, responsibilities, and habits.

Divorce means you are no longer on the same team. You have gone from being a wife or a husband to a single woman or a single man who has lost a large part of your identity. The way you define yourself and the way society defines you is changed. As one woman said, "I used to have a husband and was part of a couple. Now, I'm not only single, but a single parent as well."

Any relationship, even a difficult one, represents a sort of mirror to who you are. On many levels, it provides definition for you for what you feel, think, and hope for, and directly and indirectly provides some guidelines for how you feel about yourself and the world around you. Your marriage provided you with a point of reference to your overall identity.

"All my life I've felt like somebody's wife, or somebody's mother or somebody's daughter. Even all the time we were together, I never knew who I was."

Joanna Kramer, in *Kramer vs. Kramer*

Somewhere along your divorce journey, you may have found yourself saying something like, "I just don't feel like myself anymore." Of course you don't. You have lost a mirror that helped you know who you were. When your marriage ends, all of the structure of your life changes. You find yourself without the underpinnings of familiar rituals and habits (a morning cup of coffee or a date for the movie), and without the benefits of them. Even negative habits (fighting over finances, differences in how to discipline children) still gave you points of reference for who you were.

A divorce often requires you to take on some roles and responsibilities that had been done, or at least shared, by your former spouse. You confront your new identity every time you do something that used to be done by your husband or wife. After all, someone still has to take out the garbage, buy the groceries, and balance the checkbook. Taking on these new roles and responsibilities on your own can be very hard work and, at times, leave you feeling drained of emotional, physical and spiritual energy.

You may occasionally feel child-like as you struggle with your changed identity. You may feel a temporarily heightened dependence on others as well as feelings of helplessness, frustration, inadequacy, and fear. These feelings can be overwhelming and scary, but they are a natural response to this important need of mourning.

As you address this need, be certain to keep other major changes to a minimum if at all possible. Now is not the time for a new job or involvement in a rebound relationship. Your energy is already depleted. Don't deplete it even more by making more changes than you must or taking too many risks.

Many people find that as they work on this need, they ultimately discover some positive aspects of their changed identity. When your relationship has ended, you may realize how much of yourself you may have disowned, given away or invested in your spouse or in the relationship itself. Think of it this way: Divorce reintroduces you to yourself.

Now you have the opportunity to rediscover yourself. This discovery of parts of an old you—who you were before your marriage—and a new you can be an exciting, yet scary part of your journey. You can now dedicate yourself to being your authentic self.

You may develop a renewed confidence in yourself, for example. You may nurture the caring, kind, and sensitive part of yourself. You may develop an assertive part of your identity that empowers you to go on living. You may discover your glamorous self as you change your wardrobe. You may discover an interest in exercise and realize the importance of caring for your body. You may discover a faith community that allows you the expression of your spirituality. The list of your potential discoveries goes on and on.

Often, this rediscovery of self is a critical turning point in your pathway to healing. You have been in the wilderness of your divorce experience, and now you curiously hold up your own mirror and have some important insights into who you are and the many gifts you possess. You discover essential characteristics, inclinations, talents, and perspectives that you no longer deny. Yes, you are on a quest toward a new you. Enjoy the quest, be compassionate with yourself, and accept the support and encouragement of others. (To learn more about potential

self-identity changes that come with divorce transition, see
Touchstone Ten.)

EXPRESS YOURSELF: Go to *The Transcending Divorce
Journal*, p. 87.

Need 5: Search for Meaning

When you experience a divorce, you naturally question the
meaning and purpose of life. Yes, you will probably take a good,
hard look at your life and where you see yourself now and in the
future. You may question your philosophy of life and explore
religious and spiritual values as you work on this need. You will
instinctively revisit your account of your marriage and divorce.
"What went wrong?" "Why us?" "What could we have done
differently?" Your questions are usually part of your search. And,
I always say, those who do not search do not find.

Your former life partner was a part of you. The divorce means
you mourn a loss not only outside of yourself, but inside of
yourself as well. You may feel as if you lost part of yourself and
your sense of purpose. And now you are faced with finding some
meaning in going on with your
life even though you sometimes
feel empty and alone.

Divorce invites you to confront
your own spirituality. You
may doubt your faith and have
spiritual conflicts and questions

*"Death is not the greatest
loss in life. The greatest
loss is what dies inside
us while we live."*

Norman Cousins

racing through your head and heart. You might feel distant from
your God or Higher Power, even questioning the very existence
of God. This is normal and a part of your journey toward
renewed living.

If you do your grief work, you will see movement through this
search for meaning need and discover new life. But I have found
it cannot be hurried. Your new life vision must come in its own
time and you must allow it to unfold. It cannot be dictated or
prescribed, as much as you might wish that was not so. If you let

yourself sit with your search, which means you allow yourself to search for meaning without frantically trying to seek answers, new insights and life direction will come to you.

Even as you sit, you can also slowly begin to take an active role in your future. Part of that future can be a magical discovery, where you confront the uncertainties of your future life with an attitude of adventure. You can have hope—an expectation of a good that is yet to be—as you plan for your future.

Now you are beginning to say goodbye to many aspects of your past life and are starting to create a purposeful future life. You discover that if you are to be fully alive, you will actively live with change your whole life. Things will not remain in constant pain or constant peace. Life's journey is simply not like that. It is continually inviting movement and perturbation. If you go with it (instead of against it), actually surrender to it, you will have an amazing journey and adventure.

As you search for meaning and purpose, you are ready to make some short-term goals (next week, next month, the next six months) and some long-term goals (next year, five years from now). What is important to you in your life? How do you define success? What hopes do you have related to your work life and leisure life? Is it important to you to eventually have another love relationship? What are your financial needs and hopes and how do you accomplish them? Are you becoming the person you want to be? Every day, are you more of the person you want to be? Will you leave the world a better place? Creating new life goals is part of your search for meaning and purpose.

In an effort to discover meaning and purpose, you will benefit from trying new experiences, visiting new places, developing new ideas, and reevaluating current behaviors. In other words, you need to explore what is going to give your life purpose. What have you always dreamed of doing someday? Is there an old friend you would like to go visit? Is there a country you have always wanted to see? New meaning and purpose are revealed through exploration of what it is you want to become.

Future hopes, dreams and goals that bring meaning to your continued living can be simple or complex, short-term or long-term. Just remember: These hopes, dreams and goals have to be translated into action to impact your life. Also, keep in

"The capacity for hope is the most significant fact of life. It provides human beings with a sense of destination and the energy to get started."

Norman Cousins

mind that some old dreams might be able to be preserved with some modification. You can still watch your child go to prom. You can still walk your daughter down the aisle. You can still look forward to becoming a grandparent one day. The secret to meaning and purpose is to remember your past, put it in its proper place, and create a future that is congruent with who you are. The key is to come to know yourself as best you can and open yourself to the exploration of what you want to become. As the saying goes, "You have a choice: grow or die." I invite you to choose life!

EXPRESS YOURSELF: Go to *The Transcending Divorce Journal*, p. 89.

Need 6: Let Others Help You—Now and Always

The quality and quantity of understanding support you get during your divorce experience will have a major influence on your capacity to integrate this major transition into your life. You cannot—nor should you try to—go through this alone and in isolation. Drawing on the experiences and encouragement of friends, others who have journeyed through the wilderness of grief, or professional counselors does not mean that you are weak, only that you are meeting a healthy human need. And because divorce is a process, not an event, this support must be available over the long-term, not just during the divorce.

Unfortunately, because our society places so much value on "putting the past in the past," "moving forward" and "letting go," divorced men and women don't always receive ongoing support. "It's time to get on with your life" and "It's over and done with" and "There are more fish in the sea" are the kinds of comments that still dominate. Obviously, these messages encourage you to buck up and deny your feelings that come with this transition. People who see your experience as something that should be quickly overcome instead of experienced will not help you integrate your divorce into your life.

To be truly helpful, the people in your support system must recognize and appreciate the impact the divorce has had on you. They must understand that in order to eventually go forward in life, you must be allowed—even encouraged—to mourn your lost relationship. And they must encourage and support you *through* the painful process instead of encouraging you to go around it.

Healing from your divorce will depend not only on your inner resources but also on your surrounding support system. Your sense of who you are and where you are with your healing

"All of us, at certain moments of our lives, need to take advice and to receive help from other people."

Alexis Carrel

process comes, in part, from the care and responses of people close to you. Remember: You need not walk alone. Indeed, you cannot walk alone if you are going to heal.

You will probably discover, if you haven't already, that you can benefit from a connectedness that comes from others who have also experienced a divorce in their lives. Support groups, where people come together and share the common bond of experience, can be invaluable in helping you and supporting you as you discover your new life.

You will learn more about support groups and how to create support systems for yourself later in this book. Right now, remind yourself that you deserve and need to have understanding people around you who unconditionally support and love you as you find your way out of the dark and into the light.

EXPRESS YOURSELF: Go to *The Transcending Divorce Journal*, p. 91.

Journeying With the Six Needs

I have had the honor of supporting hundreds of people in the wilderness experience of divorce transition. During these times, I have found that most, if not all of them, have been helped by this concept of the six central needs of divorce transition. There is a lot of information in this book, but if you were to commit to memory one small piece of information, I would recommend that it be these six needs. Simply upholding and fulfilling these six needs will help you heal. I would also encourage you to revisit this chapter time and again in the future and review your progress in meeting these needs.

The Beauty of Right Now

As you actively work on these six needs, you will become open to the beauty that surrounds you right now. You can be self-compassionate and experience the capacity for joy in your life. Now you can have gratitude that you entered into the wilderness of your divorce experience. Now you can be grateful that you've discovered the meaning of life and living fully in the moment, while not being bound by your past. What a gift!

Touchstone Seven

Nurture Yourself

"Like a broken bone, the emotional wounds of divorce need to be x-rayed, reset, and given time to heal properly. The patient has to learn a new routine and is given permission to stay off her feet for a while."

Florence Littauer

I remind you that when you experience divorce, you have some special needs. Perhaps one of the most important special needs right now is to be compassionate with yourself—to honor this season of tenderness in your life. In fact, the word "compassion" means "with passion." Caring for and about yourself with passion is self-compassion.

This Touchstone is a reminder to be kind to yourself as you journey through the wilderness of your divorce. Be gentle with yourself. You are naturally fragile and vulnerable. You can give attention to your own wounds by making decisions that ultimately contribute to your healing.

If you were embarking on a hike of many days through the rugged mountains of Colorado, would you dress scantily, carry little water, and push yourself until you dropped? Of course not. You would prepare carefully and proceed cautiously. You would take care of yourself because if you didn't, you could die. The consequences of not taking care of yourself during and after your divorce can be equally devastating.

Over many years of walking with people in the wilderness of divorce, I have discovered that most of us are hard on ourselves during this time in our lives. We judge ourselves. We shame ourselves. And we often take care of ourselves last. But good self-care is essential to your survival. Practicing good self-care doesn't mean you are feeling sorry for yourself, being selfish, or being self-indulgent; rather, it means you are creating conditions that allow you to integrate the transformation that divorce brings into your heart and soul.

I believe that in nurturing ourselves, in allowing ourselves the time and loving attention we need to journey safely and deeply through the wilderness of divorce transition, we find meaning in our continued living. We have all heard the words, "Blessed are those who mourn, for they shall be comforted." I might add, "Blessed are those who learn self-compassion during times of divorce, for they shall go on to discover continued meaning in life."

Remember that self-care fortifies you during your divorce journey, a journey which leaves you profoundly affected and deeply changed. Above all, self-nurturing starts with accepting yourself. When we recognize that self-care begins with ourselves, we no longer expect or need those around us to be responsible for our well-being.

I also believe that self-nurturing is about celebration, about taking time to enjoy the moment, to find hidden treasures everywhere – a child's toothless smile, a beautiful sunrise, the smell of fresh flowers, a friend's gentle touch. The many changes that come with divorce teach us the importance of living fully in the present, remembering our past, and embracing our future.

Walt Whitman wrote, "I celebrate myself." In caring for yourself with passion, you are celebrating life as a human being who has been touched by divorce loss and has come to recognize that the preciousness of life is a superb opportunity for celebration.

Nurturing Yourself in Five Important Realms

When we have special needs, one of our most important needs is to nurture ourselves in five important areas:

• Physically

• Emotionally

• Cognitively

• Socially

• Spiritually

What follows is a brief introduction to each of these areas.

The Physical Realm

Divorce ranks among the most stressful life events you can experience. This means you have an increased risk of illness, exhaustion, and depletion of your body's resources during this time in your life. Actually, one literal definition of the word "grievous" is "causing physical suffering." You may be shocked by how much your body responds to the impact of your divorce.

Among the most common physical responses to the stress that accompanies divorce are troubles with sleeping and low energy. You may have difficulty going to sleep. Perhaps even more commonly, you may wake up early in the morning and have trouble getting back to sleep. You may find yourself getting tired more quickly. During this journey you are on, your body needs more rest than usual.

Sleeping normally as you encounter divorce would be unusual. If you think about it, sleeping is the primary way in which we release control. When you experience divorce, you feel a loss of control. You don't want to lose any more control, so your sleep is often affected. The need to stay awake sometimes relates to the fear of additional losses; therefore, you may unconsciously stay awake because you want to prevent more loss.

Muscle aches and pains, shortness of breath, feelings of emptiness in your stomach, tightness in your throat or chest, digestive problems, sensitivity to noise, heart palpitations, queasiness, nausea, headaches, increased allergies, changes in appetite, weight loss or gain, agitation, and generalized tension—these are all ways your body may react to your divorce.

If you have a chronic existing health problem, it may become worse during and after your divorce. The stress of divorce can suppress your immune system and make you more susceptible to physical problems.

"Tearless grief bleeds inwardly."

Christian Nevell Bovee

Depending on where you are right now in your divorce process, you may not feel in control of how your body is responding. Your body is communicating with you about the stress you are experiencing! Keep in mind, however, that in the majority of instances, the physical symptoms described above are normal and temporary.

Excellent self-care is important at this time. Your body is the house you live in. Just as your home requires care and maintenance to protect you from outside elements, your body requires that you honor it and treat it with respect. The quality of your life ahead depends on how you take care of your body today. The lethargy of divorce grief that you are probably experiencing is a natural mechanism intended to slow you down and encourage you to care for your body. Divorce brings an awareness of the reality that you are individually responsible for all aspects of your life, especially your health and well-being.

Caring For Your Physical Self

The following guidelines of good health are good counsel for anyone, but especially for those encountering divorce. While this is by no means an all-inclusive list, it should get you off to a good start. If you are procrastinating, adopt that now-famous Nike mantra, "Just do it!"

- *Exercise Your Heart*
  One of the best antidotes to stress is aerobic exercise. A regular program that works out your heart counteracts both the physiological and psychological toll of stress. Each day your heart beats one hundred thousand times and pumps sixteen hundred gallons of blood over sixty thousand miles of vessels. Your heart is your best friend. Support it every chance you get.

  Aerobic exercise also increases your energy level. It clears your mind and helps give you perspective on your present challenges. Also, it has been found to promote self-esteem, increase general feelings of well-being and decrease depression.

  Aerobic exercise is any activity that increases your heart rate for a continuous period of 25 minutes or longer, such as brisk walking, jogging, swimming, bicycling, or rowing. I cannot overemphasize the importance of making this kind of exercise a regular part of your lifestyle. If you do, you will probably find that you miss it on the days you don't do it.

- *Establish a Relationship with a Physician*
  Making your health a priority requires creating a relationship with a trusted physician. Do you know that some people spend more time selecting a veterinarian for their pets than they do selecting a doctor for their bodies? That's if they pick a doctor at all.

  As simple as it may seem, finding and making use of a good physician can be one of the most practical choices you can make leading to a healthier and longer life. If you have not already done so, go get a physical check-up, dental check, and eye exam. Think of your primary care physician as a coach—a trained professional—who knows how to help keep you healthy. If you don't already have one, find one now and work to create a health partnership.

- *Stay Fluid*
  Many people aren't aware that one of the easiest ways to stay healthy is to drink lots of water. Think of water as the oil that lubricates the mind and the body. Water carries oxygen, nutrients, and hormones to your cells and eliminates waste products via the bloodstream and lymphatic system. Remaining well hydrated also means having better digestion and less dry skin. The universal recommendation is six to eight glasses (10 to 12 ounces each) of water a day. Remember, caffeinated and alcoholic beverages dehydrate you, so do limit your consumption.

- *Get Adequate Sleep*
  Sleep is restorative. It allows you to live. It is a special kind of time and space. Sleep allows your mind and body the chance to perform day-to-day maintenance and repairs. While your sleep is probably disturbed in some way right now due to the stress you are experiencing, do try as best you can to get enough sleep. Determine how much you need to feel your best and then make every effort to get it.

  When possible, do try to go to bed at a similar time each night, and get up at a similar time each morning. Try to relax an hour or so before you go to bed. Limit, if not eliminate, caffeine and alcohol intake.

- *Stop Smoking Today*
  Smoking can kill you. Stopping smoking can add years to your life. The main ways smoking kills you are by heart disease, lung disease, or cancer. Smoking really is self-destructive. It's a poison, pure and simple. Tobacco kills more than 350,000 Americans every year, making it the leading cause of premature death in the United States. If you can't stop on your own, get help. You will be proud of yourself when you do stop.

- *Eat Less Fat*
  Stress places extra demands on your body, which increases your need for good nutrition and consuming less fat in your diet. Fat clogs your arteries and causes heart attacks and strokes.

Foods high in saturated fats are the worst offenders. These foods also tend to be high in cholesterol and do some of their damage by building up plaque on the walls of your arteries. These buildups are what lead to heart disease.

The reality is that the more your blood vessels are narrowed by fat and cholesterol, the less oxygen will be circulated in your body and the more fatigued you will feel. The American Heart Association recommends getting no more than 30 percent of your daily calories from fat. The less fat you consume, the better.

- *Exercise Your Muscles*
  Muscle conditioning is vitally important, yet often neglected. There are two aspects to muscle fitness: endurance and strength. In a weight-training program, lifting lighter weights with more repetitions increases endurance, while lifting heavier weights with fewer repetitions increases strength. As you age, muscle strength declines more quickly than endurance.

  The reality is that if you don't use your muscles, you will lose your muscles. If you can afford it, get help from a professional trainer to assist you in creating the right weight training program for you.

- *Slow Down, Rest and Relax*
  Are you simply too busy? Do you have to leave one commitment early to get to another? Do you feel like you always run late? If you can allow yourself to slow down, your perception of things will change. Life will become more enjoyable. You will work smarter. Instead of waiting to enjoy your life when everything is done, allow yourself to enjoy the journey.

  Set aside time every day for some rest and relaxation. I realize you may think you don't have time, but you must create time. Build in rest and relaxation—and when you do, don't feel guilty. Your times of stillness and rest are every bit as important as your times of movement and productivity. Remember, rest restores!

- *Laugh—a Lot*

  It turns out that humor is good medicine for your body, mind and spirit. Research demonstrates that laughter stimulates chemicals in the brain that actually suppress stress-related hormones. Also, respiration and circulation are both enhanced through laughter.

  In your divorce transition, you may not feel like laughing very much right now. But as the journey progresses, find ways to build laughter into your life. You might go to a live comedy show, rent a movie that makes you laugh or spend time with your funniest friend.

I hope the above guidelines related to physical self-care will help you take good care of your health. Knowing more about the needs of your body can help you design a program that best meets your unique needs. You will receive immediate results and create waves of positive energy. A personal commitment to your health paves the way for healthy self-care in the other four domains outlined below. Just as your life is being transformed right now, you can also transform your body, and re-ignite your divine spark—that which gives your life meaning and purpose.

EXPRESS YOURSELF: Go to *The Transcending Divorce Journal*, p. 96.

The Emotional Realm

We explored in Touchstone Four a multitude of emotions that are often part of the divorce journey. These emotions reflect that you often have special needs that require support from both outside yourself and inside yourself. Becoming familiar with the terrain of these emotions and practicing the self-care guidelines noted can and will help you integrate the divorce transition into your life. The important thing to remember is that we honor our emotions when we give attention to them.

Caring for Your Emotional Self

Following are just a few ideas to help you care for your emotional self during this time. We explored this extensively in Touchstone Four, but what follows are some gentle reminders to honor the emotions that come with your unique divorce journey.

- *Acknowledge and Express*
  As your experience has probably taught you, there are many feelings to be felt and expressed during this very difficult time. Feelings that go unexpressed often become painful attitudes that are self-defeating. For example, fears not expressed often become avoidance; hurt not expressed often becomes permanent sadness; anger not expressed often becomes depression.

  All feelings have some purpose. They are your teachers. So, you must find a safe place and people with whom to express them. While you have to be selective in who you express your feelings to (even some close friends will not want to experience the depth of your feelings), they do need to be converted from grief (internal) to mourning (external). Odds are this is going to be done with a counselor, a support group, selective friends, or a combination of them. This is simply a gentle reminder to be sure you honor the emotions that are part of your journey.

- *Draw a "Divorce Grief Map"*
  The divorce experience naturally stirs up all kinds of thoughts and feelings inside you. Rest assured that you're not crazy, you're grieving. Your thoughts and feelings—no matter how scary or strange they seem to you—are normal and necessary.

  Sometimes, corralling all of your varied thoughts and feelings into one place can make them feel more bearable. You could write about them, but you can also draw them out in a diagram. Make a large circle at the center of your map and label it "DIVORCE GRIEF MAP." This circle represents your thoughts and feelings connected to your divorce. Now draw lines radiating out of this circle and label each line with a thought or feeling that has contributed to your grief. For example, you might write SADNESS in a bubble at the end of one line. Next to the word SADNESS, jot down notes about why you have felt this way as part of your journey.

Your divorce grief map does not need to look pretty or follow any certain rules. The most important thing is the process of creating it. When you've finished, explain it to someone you know can be supportive to you.

- *Journal Out Your Feelings*
  Journaling can be an excellent way to give expression to your feelings. As you tell your story on paper, your words will guide you on your unique journey through the wilderness. As you know, this book actually has a companion journal titled *The Transcending Divorce Journal*. Throughout this journal you are given prompts about your own unique divorce experiences as they relate to the Touchstones outlined in this book. If you like to journal, this could be an ideal avenue for you to acknowledge and express your feelings.

- *Listen to the Music*
  Music helps many people access their feelings surrounding divorce. Music can soothe the spirit and nurture the heart. All types of music can be healing—rock & roll, classical, blues, folk. Do you play an instrument or sing? Allow yourself the time to try these means of expressing your feelings from the inside to the outside.

- *Schedule Something That Gives You Pleasure Each and Every Day*
  Often when you go through a divorce, you need something to look forward to, a reason to get out of bed each morning. To counterbalance your normal and necessary mourning around your divorce, each and every day plan, in advance, something you enjoy. Reading, baking, going for a walk, having lunch with a friend, photography, gardening—any activities that bring you enjoyment.

Increasing your pleasurable activities is an effective means of helping you with feelings of sadness, depression, and loneliness. Several studies have found that depressed people engage in very little pleasurable activity. Many people struggling with depression delay doing pleasurable things until they "feel better." The problem with that is related to how your feelings and your behaviors are connected. You see, feelings affect your behavior and your behavior affects your feelings. When you are depressed you may not feel like doing any activities (your feelings affect your behavior). However, the less you do, the more depressed you are (your behavior affects your feelings). You are now living in a vicious cycle.

Usually, if you have some feelings of sadness, depression and loneliness (which are natural with divorce transition!) and you begin to increase your pleasurable activities, you will start to feel better. Your enhanced mood will help you feel like doing more pleasurable activities. Now you have helped reverse the cycle. The key is to get started. So, make your personal list of pleasurable activities and go for it!

- *Do an Affirmation Activity*
  Some of your depressed feelings connected to divorce transition sometimes come from how you have forgotten some of the things you like about yourself and what you have going for you. Go to your companion journal right now (p. 96) and write down everything you like about yourself. (This is not a time to be humble!) Include your talents, skills, hobbies and strengths.

  Keep this list around and remind yourself of your positive attributes. Go through this list often, especially before you get together with friends or family. Doing this "attribute review" can help you in your social interactions. Remember—how you feel about yourself affects your behavior, which will influence the way people respond to you.

- *Reach Out and Touch*
  For many of us divorced folks, physical contact with another human being is healing. Touch has been recognized since ancient times as having transformative, healing powers. Have you hugged anyone lately? Been hugged by anyone lately? Held someone's hand? Put your arm around another human being?

Yes, we all need touch in our lives. Particularly when we are going through difficult times. Hug someone you feel safe with. Kiss your children or a friend's baby. Walk arm-in-arm with a friend. If you can afford it, I might recommend massage therapy. Try a session and see how it feels for you. You deserve and need to be touched in safe ways. You may be suffering from "skin hunger." So, get with it and reach out and touch someone!

EXPRESS YOURSELF: Go to *The Transcending Divorce Journal*, p. 97.

The Cognitive Realm

Your mind has the intellectual ability to think, absorb information, make decisions and reason logically. Without doubt, the divorce experience will impact you in the cognitive realm. Just as your body and emotions let you know you have special needs, your mind does too.

Being able to consistently think normally when impacted by divorce would be very unlikely. Don't be surprised if you struggle with short-term memory problems, have trouble making even simple decisions and think you may be going crazy. Essentially, your mind is in a state of disorientation and confusion.

"Grief teaches the steadiest minds to waver."

Sophocles

Caring For Your Cognitive Self

The following are some practical ideas to help you care for your cognitive self as you encounter your divorce experiences. Your mind needs time to catch up with what you are experiencing. Be gentle with yourself right now and don't expect too much of yourself in this cognitive area of functioning.

- *When Possible, Do Not Make Impulsive Major Decisions During This Time*

While it can be helpful to have goals to help you look to a brighter future, it can be a mistake to make too many changes too quickly. Divorce often sets off "fight or flight" responses. Sometimes, in an effort to get away from pain, you can be tempted to make rash decisions. Some people move to a new city or quit their jobs. Some people jump into new relationships too quickly.

Typically these changes are soon regretted. They often end up compounding feelings of loss and complicating healing as well as creating staggering new headaches.

If at all possible (and I realize it isn't always possible), avoid making additional major changes for a while. After all, you are already experiencing a huge change with additional layers of change and loss. You cannot run away from the pain, so don't make it worse by trying to.

Of course, sometimes you may be forced to make a significant change in your life after your divorce. Financial realities may force you to sell your home, for example. In these cases, know that you are doing what you must and try to trust as best you can that everything will work out.

- *Simplify Your Life*
  During the cognitive confusion of divorce, it is easy to get overwhelmed by the daily tasks and commitments you have. Divorce can really make you take stock of what is important in your life. If you can rid yourself of some of these extraneous burdens, you'll have more time for healing.

  What are some things that might be overburdening you right now? For example, have your name taken off junk mailing lists, don't make yourself stressed out because your house isn't always sparkling clean and neat, stop attending optional meetings you don't look forward to.

- *Write Things Down*
  Your short-term memory is impaired right now. So, help yourself out and write things down. A brief daily to-do list can help you focus during this difficult time. (Oh, and then make a list of where you put your list because you will probably forget

where you put it. I hope that brought a little laugh to you! A little laughter is good for your soul right now.)

- *Say No and Set Limits*
When your cognitive capacity and physical energy are compromised, you may lack the psychic energy to participate in activities you used to find pleasurable. It's okay to say no when you're asked to help with a project or attend a party.

Give a brief phone call to people who have invited you and simply thank them for the invite but say no. You don't need to feel obligated to go on and on and explain why. You have the right to say no.

Do recognize that you will not be able to keep saying no forever. There will be some events you won't want to miss. Don't miss out on life's most joyful celebrations. However, trust your sense of when the time is right for you to rejoin in the occasions.

- *Keep a Journal*
If you like to write out your thoughts and feelings, journaling is an excellent tool to help keep you oriented during a time of natural disorientation. Similar to how you might sometimes talk out loud to yourself in an effort to see if you make sense, journaling helps you focus when it is difficult to feel totally tuned in to what you are thinking and feeling. In addition to the journal that accompanies this book, you might consider keeping a blank book on your nightstand for writing down your spontaneous thoughts and feelings.

- *Practice Patience*
Your normal cognitive abilities take longer to return after a divorce than most people are aware. So, you need to be patient and gentle with yourself. Our society, which promotes hyper-living, is constantly trying to speed things up. However, your confused, slow-thinking mind has wisdom and is trying to slow you down because this is what you need right now. Patience is the ability to endure or to persevere with a calm heart during difficult moments. It was Helen Keller who wisely reminded us that, "We could never learn to be patient or brave

if there were only joy in the world." So, take each and every opportunity given to you to practice becoming more patient with yourself and your divorce experience. Practicing patience opens your mind and heart to the present moment and allows healing and joy into your life.

- *Take Some Time Off Work*
  I realize there is no such thing as "divorce leave," but if you can get some time off work without the risk of losing your job, this is a good time to do so. Talk to your supervisor about taking off some additional time or using some vacation time. Some companies will grant extended leaves of absence or sabbaticals in some situations. If you simply can't take off additional time, try not to take on new challenges that will further task your concentration and memory right now. Instead of taking on more, just try to survive in your workplace for a while. Over time your focus will return, and you will be able to perform well in your job.

- *Take a Bubble Bath or Hot Tub*
  When your mind feels dazed, it needs some really good self-care. In our hurried world, showers are usually the order of the day. We often don't allow time for the pleasure of a long, hot, bubble bath.

  You will be well served to draw an occasional hot, hot bath. Pour in some bath salts, oils or bubbles. Place candles around the bathroom (safely!). Turn off all of the overhead lights and simply relax and enjoy. Soak until the water grows tepid. Clear your mind and focus on the sensation of the water lapping around you.

  Oh, and for you guys who are thinking this sounds way too feminine for you—go jump in a hot tub and enjoy!

- *Practice Breathing In and Out*
  Sometimes when your mind is overwhelmed, what you need most is just to "be." You will probably find some value in what is called *autogenic breathing*. It is fairly simple, yet effective in helping you relax your mind, body and spirit.

All you have to do is breathe in very deeply for four full seconds, and hold it for two seconds. Then slowly release your breath for four seconds, and hold for two additional seconds. Then repeat.

You can do this any place, any time. The more often you can build time in to do this the better. Try for a minimum of 10 minutes a couple of times each day. Odds are you will notice how calm and relaxed this makes you feel, both mentally and physically.

- *Take a Mini-Vacation*
  With all the stress your mind and heart are under, you will benefit from a mini-vacation. You can probably think of a number of reasons you don't have time for an extended vacation, so consider a mini-vacation. You need it and you deserve it!

What creative ideas can you come up with to renew yourself? Since you are not thinking sharply right now, here are a few ideas for you to consider:

1. Go for a drive with no particular destination in mind, going slowly and observing what you see.

2. Treat yourself to a night in a hotel or bed and breakfast.

3. Schedule a session with a massage therapist.

4. Visit a museum or a zoo.

5. Go to a yard sale or an auction.

6. Go to a park and simply take a walk or relax.

7. Go for a bike ride.

8. Do a small amount of "retail" therapy. In other words, go shopping, but don't overspend.

9. Meet an old friend for a weekend getaway.

10. Simply plan to "be" for a few days and have no plans or commitments.

EXPRESS YOURSELF: Go to *The Transcending Divorce Journal*, p. 101.

The Social Realm

Naturally, divorce can sometimes leave you feeling disconnected from the outside world. Having a support system of friends and family you can count on is vital. When you reach out and connect with friends and family, you are beginning to reconnect. By being aware of the larger picture, one that includes all the people in your life, you gain some perspective. You recognize you are part of a greater whole, and that recognition can empower you. Your link to family, friends, and community is essential for your sense of well-being and belonging.

If you don't nurture the warm, loving relationships that still exist in your life, you run the risk of feeling disconnected and isolated. Some people withdraw into their own small worlds and end up grieving the divorce, but not mourning. I don't want that to be you! Isolation can then

"Friendship doubles our joy and divides our grief."
Swedish Proverb

become the barrier that keeps you from integrating your divorce into your life. Then you risk beginning to die inside while you are still very much alive. Allow select friends and family to nurture you. Let them in and rejoice in the connection.

Caring for Your Social Self

The following are some practical ideas to help you care for your social self during your divorce journey.

- *Recognize That Your Friendships Will Probably Change*
  You may well find that some friends seem to go away during this time in your life. Know that just like you, your friends are doing the best they can. Don't be surprised if some of your friends cannot even talk with you about your divorce. For some, your reality is a threat to their potential reality. Instead of acknowledging their own fears, they feel a need to go away and not talk to you. Yes, this is sad, but often true.

  Some people, including members of your family and friendship system, may not be able to be present to you in the wilderness of your divorce. Divorce makes some people feel very awkward and uncomfortable. They may not even be conscious of this reaction, but nonetheless, it affects their ability to support you. Limit your time around family and friends who cannot be supportive to you.

The best way for you to respond in the face of strained relationships is to be proactive and honest. Even though you are the one who is in the wilderness, you may need to be the one to phone your family and friends to keep in touch. When you talk to them, be honest. Tell them how you're really feeling and that you appreciate any support they can provide you. If you find that certain people can't handle your divorce talk, stick to lighter topics with them and look for support from people whom you learn are capable of giving it. Put yourself in the company of warm-hearted, non-judgmental people who help you feel accepted and cared for.

Over time, you will probably notice a natural attrition among your friends. Some may pick sides and stay friends with your spouse, but not you. You will need to mourn these losses, though you will likely also find that other friendships deepen and new ones emerge.

By contrast, maybe you are one of the fortunate ones who feel tremendous support and love from your family and friends related to your divorce. If so, rejoice that you have such wise and wonderful people surrounding you.

- *Turn To Select Family Members*
  If you ever needed to embrace the gift of having some loving, caring family members, it is right now. Your friends may come and go, but family, as they say, is forever. If you're emotionally close to members of your family, you're probably already reaching out to them for support. Allow them to be there for you. Let them in.

  If you're not emotionally close to your family, perhaps now is the time to open closed doors. You may be surprised what happens when you call a family member you haven't spoken to for a while. If possible, get in the car or on a plane and make a long-overdue visit. Don't feel bad if you have to be the initiator; instead, expend your energy by writing that first letter or making that first phone call.

- *Identify Two People You Can Turn To Anytime You Need A Friend*
You may have many people who care about you but few people who can truly be present to you at this time in your life. Identify and stay conscious of two people whom you believe can and will be there for you in the coming weeks and months. Have gratitude for their support and let them know how much it means to you.

- *Reach Out To Counselors, Support Groups, And Additional Resources*
Sometimes you need more structured support than your friends and family can provide. To seek social support from these domains is the very heart of Touchstone Eight, "Reach Out for Help." Please see this information on pp. 159-168.

- *Find A Way To Connect To Others Or To Nature Each And Every Day*
When you are in the wilderness of divorce and impacted in this social area of your life, it may be difficult to look forward to each day when you are experiencing pain and sadness. So, to counterbalance your normal and necessary mourning of lost dreams, plan something you enjoy doing and that will help you to connect to others every day.

- *Brighten Up Your Environment*
Would you enjoy sprucing up your living space a little? Paint your living room or bedroom in a fresh, new color. Paint is fairly inexpensive and easy to redo. Sometimes something as minor as new valances and clean windows can make a big difference. Or, maybe a few new throw pillows with colors you enjoy. Place some fresh flowers somewhere you will see them throughout the day. You might also enjoy watching the TV network HGTV or buying a decorating magazine, which can inspire you with some new ideas to decorate your environment.

EXPRESS YOURSELF: Go to *The Transcending Divorce Journal*, p. 103.

The Spiritual Realm

I realize that the word spiritual has many different meanings to different people. For our purposes here, I think of spiritual as the collection of beliefs that make sense of our existence. Divorce naturally invites you into some spiritual questions for which there are no easy answers: Why did this happen to me? Why did my marriage have to end this way? Where did things go wrong? Will life be worth living again?

Your spiritual encounter with divorce often invites new questions about your past, your present, and your future. You naturally go on a search to understand your lost relationship and may discover a perspective that places life in the context of something bigger than your day-to-day existence. Once you have discovered your spiritual core, you will have an undergirding strength that will support your wilderness experience.

My own personal source of spirituality anchors me, allowing me to put my life into perspective. For me, spirituality involves a sense of connection to all things in nature, God, and the world at large. I recognize that, for some, contemplating a spiritual life in the midst of divorce can be difficult.

Yet life is a miracle, and we need to remind ourselves of that, during both happy times and sad times. When it comes to our spiritual lives, we have an abundance of choices, all of which can be doors leading to the soul. Spirituality can be found in simple things: a sunrise or sunset; the unexpected kindness of a stranger; the rustle of the wind in the trees.

If you have doubts about your capacity to connect with God and the world around you, try to approach the world with the openness of a child. Embrace the pleasure that comes from the simple sights, smells, and sounds that greet your senses. You can and will find yourself rediscovering the essentials within your soul and the spirit of the world around you.

Nurturing a spiritual life invites you to connect with nature and the people around you. Your heart opens and your life takes on renewed meaning and purpose. You are filled with compassion for other people, particularly those who have walked the path of divorce. You become kinder, gentler, and more forgiving of others as well as yourself.

Caring for Your Spiritual Self

The following are some practical ideas to help you care for your spiritual self during this time in your life.

- *Express Your Faith/Spirituality In A Body Of Community*
  As you know, divorce can challenge your physical health, your emotional well-being, and your spiritual sense of vitality. The wilderness experience of divorce can drain the energy out of you, and you will benefit from sources that help replenish it. One of the places you may find that help to refuel you is your spiritual community.

  Attending a church, synagogue, temple or other place of worship, reading religious texts and praying are a few conventional ways of expressing your faith. If these ways of expressing bring meaning to you, by all means make use of them. Expressing yourself in the body of a spiritual community is also acknowledging you are surrounded by a personal community of people who care about you.

  > *"We need to find God, and he cannot be found in noise and restlessness. God is the friend of silence. See how nature—trees, flowers, grass—grows in silence; see the stars, the moon and the sun, how they move in silence...We need silence to be able to touch souls."*
  >
  > Mother Teresa

  Reflect for a moment on how you express your faith/ spirituality in a body of community. Consider their importance and value to you. What role will you allow those with whom you share spiritual practices to play in your life during this challenging time? Community can help you counter any tendency you might have to over-isolate yourself. Remember, divorce is a spiritual journey of the heart and soul that benefits from a sense of community. Find your personal community and give expression to your faith and spirituality.

- *Create A Sacred Space Of Sanctuary*
Creating a sacred, safe space—a sanctuary—just for you may be one of the most loving ways you can help yourself at this time. Yes, you need the loving support of friends, family and community, but nurturing yourself during difficult times can also involve going to exile.

Whether it is indoors or out, give yourself a place for spiritual contemplation. The word contemplate means "to make space for the divine to enter." Think of your space, if only a simple room, as a place dedicated exclusively to the needs of the soul. Retreat to your space seven times a week and honor your journey through divorce.

- *Start Each Day With A Prayer Or Meditation*
For many people in the wilderness of divorce, waking up in the morning can be a difficult part of the day. It's as if each time you awaken, you confront the realization of the loss of your relationship.

You may find that you can help set the tone for your day by praying or meditating. Prayer and meditation are some of the easiest spiritual practices you can do any time, any place, any way. You might not only experience some wisdom that comes from these practices, but also experience the peace that comes from spending quiet, reflective time with God.

Some people think of prayer as a practice directed at petitioning God for what they want. Try viewing prayer differently: See it as a practice that aims to change your life not by divine intervention, but by creating a more humble spirit in you. The purpose of prayer is to change you, not the circumstances surrounding your divorce experience.

- *Name Your Gratitude And Count Your Blessings*
You may not be feeling very good about your life right now. You may feel you are unlucky. You may feel you are destined to be alone and unhappy. That's okay. There is, indeed, a time for every purpose under heaven, including self-doubt. Indeed, self-doubt can be a normal part of your divorce experience.

Still, you are blessed. Your life has purpose and meaning. It may just take you some time to think and feel this through for yourself. This is not to deny your hurt, but it may help to consider things that make your life worth living, too.

Think of all you have to be thankful for. When you choose to have gratitude in your life, you come to realize that everything you receive is a gift. If you see your life through a lens of entitlement, you cannot open yourself to your "gifts of gratitude." You experience gratitude when you look at all you have instead of what you don't have. Open your heart and count your blessings.

- *Savor The Silence*
Mother Teresa often said, "The beginning of prayer is silence." It takes practice to be silent, to allow the divine to speak in the quiet of your open heart. Today, be silent for a while—silent with God or with yourself. This may be a difficult spiritual practice, but certainly one that is worth the effort. Remember: Mouth closed, ears open!

- *Celebrate A Sunrise*
The sun is a powerful symbol of life and renewal. When was the last time you watched the sun rise? Do you remember being touched by its beauty and power? Plan an early morning experience where you can see the sun rise. Find a place that offers you a great view. You may need to go alone or invite a supportive friend to share the dawn with you. Embrace your personal transformation and feel blessed by the dawning of a new day, a new life!

- *Know That You Are Loved*
Love gives our lives meaning. Look around you for expressions of care and concern. There are people who love you and want to be an important part of your support system.

Yes, some of those who love you may not know how to reach out to you, but they still love you. Reflect on the people who care about you and the ways in which your life matters. Open your heart and have gratitude for those who love you.

155

- *Visit The Great Outdoors*
  For many people, it is restorative and energizing to spend time outside. Nature's timeless beauty can be naturally healing. The sound of a bird singing or the awesome presence of an old tree can help put things in perspective.

  Go on a nature walk. Or camping. Or canoeing. The farther away from civilization the better. Mother Earth knows more about relaxing than all of the stress-management experts on the planet—and she charges far less.

  What is your favorite outdoor getaway? It may be as awesome as a mountain peak or as simple as your own backyard. Wherever it is, go there if you can.

- *Find A Spiritual Director*
  A spiritual director or spiritual companion is someone who is trained in compassionate listening who will support you in your journey. You can find sources near you by going to www. sdiworld.org (Spiritual Directors International). Don't be afraid to try several spiritual directors until you find the person who connects with you.

- *Sigh*
  In Romans 8, it says that when there are not words for our prayer, the Spirits intervene and pray for us in sighs deeper than anything that can be expressed in words. Sigh deeply. Sigh whenever you feel like it. Each sigh is your prayer.

- *Create A Divorce Ceremony*
  Most major events in our lives have some kind of ceremony to acknowledge them—with the exception of divorce. Fortunately, a recent trend is seeing more people participate in healing divorce ceremonies. As I always say, "When words are inadequate, have a ceremony."

  Divorce ceremonies often include blame-eliminating statements and acknowledge mutual responsibility for the ending of the relationship, in addition to mutual goodwill for the future. They often close with the Serenity Prayer.

An excellent source for ceremony ideas can be found in the book titled *A Healing Divorce* by Phil and Barbara Penningroth (ISBN 1-58721-793-7). This book demonstrates how ceremony can transform and heal the end of a relationship. The thought is, and I agree, the more conscious a parting and the more healing a divorce, the more life-affirming the end of a relationship will be for individuals, families, and the world.

EXPRESS YOURSELF: Go to *The Transcending Divorce Journal*, p. 105.

Practicing Self-Compassion

We've explored five realms of self-care during this naturally difficult time in your life: physical, emotional, cognitive, social, and spiritual. If you care for yourself "with passion" in all five realms, you will find your journey through the wilderness of divorce much more tolerable. So be good to yourself. For some guidance and reassurance about your right to be self-compassionate, see "The Divorced Person's Bill of Rights," p. 193.

Finding others who will be good to you is also critically important. You can't walk this path alone. In the next chapter, I'll help you construct a plan to reach out for help.

Touchstone Eight

Reach Out for Help

"Action is the antidote to despair."
Joan Baez

Yes, I have said that the wilderness of your divorce grief is *your* wilderness, and it's up to you to find your way through it. That's true. But, paradoxically, you also need companionship from time to time as you journey. I believe everyone involved in a divorce requires support and understanding through this naturally difficult time.

During this challenging time of major transition in your life, nothing can take the place of a caring community of supportive others. You need people who will walk beside you and provide you with "divine momentum"—affirmation that what you are doing is right and necessary for you and will lead to your eventual healing. You do *not* need people who want to walk in front of you and lead you down the path they think is right, nor do you need people who want to walk behind you and not be present to your pain.

"There is strength in numbers," one saying goes. Another echoes, "United we stand, divided we fall." In your divorce wilderness experience, you may indeed find strength and a sense of stability if you build and then draw on an entire support system for help.

No, sharing your challenges with others won't make them disappear, but it will, over time, make them more bearable. Reaching out for help also connects you to other people and strengthens the bonds of love that make life worth living.

Carefully selected friends and family members can often form the core of your support system. Reach out to others. Do not make the mistake of totally withdrawing because you don't want to "burden" people. Look for family and friends who can provide you non-judgmental support. The caring, warmth, and support of others goes a long way in cushioning the impact of the stresses and challenges that come with divorce. Sometimes, a few compassionate people who are gifted with effective listening ears can make all the difference in the world. Who can you discern has this capacity among your friends and family?

> *"Life is to be fortified by many friendships. To love and be loved is the greatest happiness of existence."*
>
> Sydney Smith

A word of caution: In an ideal world, you would get the non-judgmental support I'm describing from your family and friends. If this is not true for you, I encourage you to seek out other sources of support; get help from somebody else. Don't play the role of victim if your existing family and friends are not able to be supportive to you.

Actually, getting support from family members can sometimes be difficult, if not impossible. Some family members are too quick to offer their advice and give opinions than to unconditionally support you. When you are going through a divorce, your family sometimes feels like a pressure cooker. After all, your family members also have feelings about your ex, sometimes good, sometimes bad. They often experience a sense of needing to be understood, but may have little capacity to be understanding to you. Beyond this, some family members just have a natural gift for saying the wrong thing at the wrong time! In my situation, it has often been my mother—though I still love her and always will. Do you have any of these people in your family? Odds are that you do, and you are faced with loving them, but not always liking them.

The implication of what I'm describing here is this: Don't assume that everyone in your family and friendship system will be capable of loving and supporting you through this experience. Expand your network beyond these people to other sources of support.

You've heard me urge you over and over again in this book to seek out the support of the people in your life who are naturally good helpers. Perhaps

"A friend is one who walks in when others walk out."

Walter Winchell

you have been blessed with a consistent network of supportive friends and family members (if only this were true for all of us!), plus the self-motivation to do the emotional and spiritual work you need to do on your own, and you feel that this is enough. But for others, perhaps most of us, professional supportive counseling with someone who understands that grief is a core part of the divorce journey can be very beneficial.

One other caveat related to seeking support: Be careful not to express what you are going through to everyone and anyone all the time. Your divorce is a process you are going through, and you can't expect everyone to be able to be present to you during your journey. In addition, your divorce is not the core of your identity or lifestyle. If you find yourself talking with everyone and anyone about your divorce and seeking their support, I encourage you to see a professional counselor who can help you sort out what you are experiencing. If you don't seek additional help, some of your family and friends may begin to avoid you, and the result will be that you feel rejected or abandoned. The last thing you need to feel right now is a sense of abandonment.

Dr. Wolfelt's "Rule of Thirds"

In my own divorce experience and in the lives of people I have been privileged to counsel, I have discovered that in general, you can take all the people in your life and divide them into thirds when it comes to grief support.

One third of the people in your life will turn out to be neutral in response to your divorce experience. They will neither help nor hinder you in your journey.

Another third of the people in your life will turn out to be harmful to you in your efforts to integrate the divorce into your life. While they are usually not setting out to intentionally harm you, they will judge you, give you unsolicited advice about what you should do, minimize your experience, "buck you up," or, in general, just try to pull you off your path to eventual healing and transcendence.

And the final third of people in your life will turn out to be truly supportive helpers. They will demonstrate a desire to understand you and the experience you are going through. They will demonstrate a willingness to be taught by you and recognize that you are the expert of your experience, not them. They will be willing to be involved in your pain and suffering without feeling the need to take it away from you. They will believe in your capacity to integrate this divorce into your life and eventually go on to live a life of meaning and purpose.

Obviously, you want to seek out your friends and family who fall into this last third. They will be your confidants and momentum-givers on your journey. When you are in the wilderness of divorce transition, try to avoid that second third, for they will trip you up and cause you to fall. They may even light up a wildfire right there in the midst of your wilderness!

EXPRESS YOURSELF: Go to *The Transcending Divorce Journal*, p. 110.

Safe People: Three Fundamental Helping Roles

While there are a multitude of ways that people who care about you might reach out to help you, here are three important and fundamental helping roles. Effective helpers will help you:

1. Feel companioned during your journey. Someone who companions you is someone who is willing and able to affirm your pain and suffering. They are able to sit with you and the feelings that surface as you walk through the wilderness. They are able to break through their separation from you and truly companion you where you are at

"I get by with a little help from my friends."

John Lennon

this moment in time. They know that real compassion comes out of "walking with you," not ahead of you or behind you.

2. Encounter your feelings related to the divorce transition. These are people who understand the need for you to tell your account of your marriage and divorce. They ask you about your story and provide a safe place for you to openly express your many thoughts and feelings. Essentially, they give you an invitation to take any grief that is inside you and share it outside yourself.

3. Embrace hope. These are people around you who help you sustain the presence of hope—an expectation of good that is yet to be—even when you are in the middle of the wilderness of your divorce. They can be present to you and affirm your goodness, while all the time helping you trust in yourself that you can and will heal.

EXPRESS YOURSELF: Go to *The Transcending Divorce Journal*, p. 111.

Seeking Outside Help from a Counselor

A professional counselor may be a very helpful addition to your support system. There is no shame or weakness in seeing a counselor. On the contrary, it takes wisdom to realize you would benefit from this kind of help. A professional caregiver can sometimes help you look at areas you might like to avoid and give you some positive, objective counsel.

Since this is a naturally vulnerable time for you, however, you do need to use your discernment skills to find the right therapist for you. Try to find someone whom you connect and resonate with. You will know you may have found the right counselor when you feel safe, can be open and honest, and your spirit feels "at home."

In selecting a counselor (keep in mind they might have different job titles, ranging from psychologist to psychiatrist,

"We may define therapy as a search for value."

Abraham Maslow

social worker, family therapist or counselor), you have the right to ask questions. After all, you deserve someone who is best matched to your needs.

- *Training, Philosophy, Experience*
  As you explore your options, feel free to ask about the counselor's education and training. What degrees has she earned? What certificates or licenses does he hold? Reputable professionals will feel comfortable answering questions about their training, philosophy and experience. Be certain the person you are seeing specializes in divorce-related issues. Even highly qualified professionals may not have experience working with divorce transition. If he or she hasn't worked in this area, keep looking.

- *Relationship*
  While this is a very subjective area, the question is: Does the person seem like someone you would be able to work with effectively? Does her personality, answers to your questions and concerns, and office environment make you feel safe and respected? Do you sense that he genuinely cares about you as a human being and about the work you are going to be doing together? Essentially, do you feel comfortable with this person and sense that she can help you? If it does not feel right, then it is probably not right for you.

Some excellent, short-term counseling with the right person can give you insights and tools that will be invaluable to you during this difficult time in your life. No, most people who go through the transition of divorce don't require long-term therapy. A gentle, short course of counseling, with the right match for you, can be a life-changing experience and a vital step on your healing path.

EXPRESS YOURSELF: Go to *The Transcending Divorce Journal*, p. 111.

Spiritual Sources of Support and Counsel

One of the fastest-growing sources of support for divorced people is the assistance found in many spiritual communities. Churches, synagogues and other spiritual groups offer a variety of resources that may be of help to you, ranging from individual counseling, to classes, workshops and support groups. Some are affiliated with national organizations like "Beginning Experience" or "Divorce Care," and some are not.

While some of these programs are anchored in a specific religious tradition, many are open to people of any faith, not just members of the host organization. Also, it is important to realize that not all of the divorce services offered by faith communities are spiritually based or faith-based; some are completely secular, the only connection being the physical space where meetings take place. Many of these programs are non-denominational and reach out in a way that honors diversity. Also, many of these programs are available for free or at a very low cost, accepting donations or waiving costs altogether if you cannot afford to pay.

If your religious faith or spirituality is a vital source of comfort to you, you may be well served to seek out sources of support in these kinds of settings. Again, just be a wise and discerning shopper. Find a place you feel at home, understood and non-judged. Spiritual support may be just what you need to put things in perspective, get practical assistance, and restore your faith in a future filled with gratitude and hope.

"I always love to begin a journey on Sundays, because I shall have the prayers of the church, to preserve all that travel by land, or by water."

Jonathan Swift

EXPRESS YOURSELF: Go to *The Transcending Divorce Journal*, p. 112.

How Do I Know if I Need Professional Help?

It is not always easy to tell yourself you need professional help. Yet, if you are asking yourself this question and suspect you do need some help, go get it as soon as possible. The lingering pain of divorce can affect your self-esteem, ability to trust, physical health, career, finances, and the list goes on. These are not insignificant matters and should not be ignored. Admitting you need some help is a sign of strength. A skilled professional can sometimes help facilitate the six needs of divorce transition (Touchstone Six) outlined in this book and affirm that you are doing the right things to help yourself heal.

Having encouraged anyone and everyone to seek counseling for this major life transition, do let me go over some "Red Flags" where I believe professional assistance is necessary:

- Deep depression that never eases up

- Anxiety disorders, accompanied by panic attacks

- A consistent lack of caring about one's self and one's future; profound hopelessness

- An inability to provide basic care to dependent children

- High-risk, self-destructive behavior, including any suicidal thoughts and plans

- Excessive overindulgence in alcohol, drugs, food, gambling

- Hyper-sexuality with lack of boundaries and premature involvement in new relationships

- Using children as a weapon against your former spouse

- Lingering feelings toward your former spouse that are blocking your personal growth

- Harassing or stalking your ex, or behaving in ways that could be considered abusive toward another person, particularly your children

- A consistent pattern of real or imagined physical illness

If you meet any of the criteria outlined, I ask you to please seek professional assistance immediately.

EXPRESS YOURSELF: Go to *The Transcending Divorce Journal*, p. 112.

Support Groups

You will probably discover, if you haven't already, that you can benefit from connecting with people who have also gone through a divorce. This "been there" factor is often the greatest benefit of divorce support groups. Coming together and sharing the common bond of experience can be invaluable in helping you heal. Knowing you are not alone when you feel like you are going crazy provides support and comfort.

In these groups, each person can talk about his or her experience in a non-threatening, safe atmosphere. Members offer each other support based on real life experience. Group members are usually very patient with you, and since they are not friends or family, can often have some outside perspective that is helpful to you.

You might think of divorce support groups as places where fellow journeyers gather. Each of you has a story to tell. Your wilderness stories help affirm the normalcy of each other's experiences. You also help each other build divine momentum toward healing.

"The most I can do for my friend is simply to be his friend. I have no wealth to bestow on him. If he knows that I am happy in loving him, he will want no other reward. Is not friendship divine in this?"

Henry David Thoreau

Divorce support groups are available in many communities. They vary tremendously in their formats (open versus closed), duration, and content. If you are a candidate for one of these groups, do your research and find one that best meets your needs. While groups can be helpful, they are not for everyone. If in doubt, find a trusted confidant or counselor who can help you explore if this kind of experience might be of help to you.

To find a support group in your area, call your local mental health agency. Also, clergy, physicians, and attorneys will sometimes know about groups in your area.

EXPRESS YOURSELF: Go to *The Transcending Divorce Journal*, p. 113.

Additional Resources

A variety of resources related to divorce are available to assist you. These include a multitude of books, newsletters, magazines, and Internet resources. As you may know, having a computer is like having an online library. Many divorce groups and organizations maintain websites filled with good information. Do weigh what you come across on the Web against your own experience and common sense, however. Yes, there are many resources you can access that fit within the realm of "Reaching Out for Help" emphasized in this chapter. Do reach out, but use discernment in what you reach out and find.

EXPRESS YOURSELF: Go to *The Transcending Divorce Journal*, p. 113.

A Final Word About Reaching Out for Help

As a counselor, I have been honored to have many people who are going through or have gone through a divorce reach out to me for help. Among other important lessons, they have taught me that seeking support from others is an integral part of the healing process.

I hope this Touchstone has helped you understand the importance of reaching out for help when you are grieving. Please don't try to journey through the wilderness of your divorce alone. You need companions—friends, family, counselors, others who have experienced divorce—who will walk with you as you move toward healing and transcendence.

Touchstone Nine

Seek Integration—Not Resolution

*"Your life changes the moment you make a
new, congruent, and committed decision."*

Anthony Robbins

How do you find your way out of the wilderness of your divorce
experience? You don't have to dwell there forever, do you?

The good news is that the answer is no, you don't have to
dwell there forever. Throughout this book, while exploring the
misconceptions and realities of divorce, I have provided you
with some trail markers on your journey *through* the wilderness.
Along the way, my hope is that you have truly felt my optimism,
hope, and belief in your courage and capacity to make it through
your challenges and transitions. The good news is that like the
millions who have gone before you, you can and will find your
way out. But just as with any significant experience in your life,
from this point forward this wilderness journey will always be a
part of who you are and it will influence who you will become in
the future.

Women and men who are in the process of divorce are often told
to "resolve" the end of the relationship and "let go." As a matter

of fact, a number of models of divorce adjustment describe end goals with terms like "resolution," "recovery," "reestablishment," or "reorganization." You may have heard—actually, you may believe—that your divorce journey's end will come when you resolve, or recover from, your divorce.

But you may also be coming to understand one of the fundamental truths of the encounter with divorce transition: You don't wake up one day and magically feel "over it." Even when you do emerge from the wilderness, you are forever changed and transformed by the experience.

> *"It isn't for the moment you are struck that you need courage, but for the long uphill battle to faith, sanity and security."*
>
> Anne Morrow Lindbergh

Integration is a term I find more appropriate for what occurs as you work to embrace the new reality of moving forward in life without your former spouse. With integration comes an ability to fully acknowledge the end of your marriage, feeling and acting like a single person with a future of your own design, a renewed sense of energy and confidence, and a capacity to become re-involved in the activities of life. There is also an acknowledgment of any feelings of loss, sadness, protest, relief (emotions outlined in Touchstone Four), even as you no longer harbor them or allow them to control you.

As the experience of integration unfolds, you will recognize that life is and will continue to be different without the presence of your former life partner. Your changed relationship from presence to memory and redirecting your energy and initiative toward the future often takes longer—and involves more hard work—than most people are aware. I propose that as human beings we never totally resolve our divorce experiences, but instead, we integrate them into our lives, and are forever changed by them.

While it is natural to prefer that your divorce could be wrapped up in some neat, clean package and completely resolved, my experience with thousands of people has taught me otherwise.

Actually, to integrate your divorce into your new life means, in part, accepting that there may be some feelings that remain unresolved and ambiguous. You may naturally need to do some aspects of catch-up mourning even years later. But, that's okay, and you can and will be able to do it. You will be able to integrate your past with your present.

Integration of your divorce journey goes beyond an intellectual working through of the reality of the end of the relationship. There is also an emotional and spiritual working through. Yes, there is a difference between your legal divorce and your emotional and spiritual divorce. What had been understood at the head level is now integrated and understood at the heart level.

The Resolution Wish

We wish that grief would resolve. We wish that it was linear and finite. We wish that we could wake up one day and our painful thoughts and feelings would all be "over." Grief never resolves, however. While we can learn to reconcile ourselves to it, grief is transformative and life-changing.

Keep in mind that this process of integration does not just happen. It requires that you *descend* before you *transcend*. You don't go around, under, or over your wilderness experience. You must go through it. You must intentionally express it if you are to integrate it into your new and changed life.

You will find that as you embrace this process of integration, the upheaval that comes with the wilderness will give rise to a new sense of meaning and purpose. Hope for a continued life will emerge as you are able to make commitments to your future. You can create a hopeful attitude and discover a desire to live a full life filled with gratitude and peace.

"Healing takes courage, and we all have courage, even if we have to dig a little to find it."

Tori Amos

171

Signs of Integration

To help you explore where you are in your movement toward integration, the following signs that suggest healing may be helpful to you. You don't have to see each and every one of the signs for healing to be taking place. Again, remember that integration is an ongoing process. If you are early in your divorce experience, you may not have found any of these signs yet in your journey. But this list will give you a way to monitor your movement ("perturbation") toward healing. You may want to place checkmarks beside those signs you believe you know are present in your journey thus far.

As you integrate your divorce into your life, you can and will be able to demonstrate the majority of the following:

- A willingness to acknowledge that the divorce is happening (reality of the divorce) and that your relationship as a couple is over (finality of the divorce).

- A return to stable eating and sleeping patterns.

- Feeling and acting like a single person with a future of your own. You will have thoughts of your former spouse, but you will not be preoccupied by these thoughts.

- The capacity to enjoy experiences in life that are normally enjoyable.

- The establishment of both old and new friendships.

- The desire and capacity to makes plans for your future and look forward to what awaits you.

- The desire and capacity to plan your life toward the future.

- The serenity to become comfortable with the way things are rather than attempting to make things as they were.

- The versatility to welcome more change in your life.

- The awareness that you have allowed yourself to fully mourn, and you are still breathing—you have survived.

- The awareness that you don't completely "resolve" or "get over" your divorce; instead, you integrate it into your life.

- The acquaintance of new parts of yourself that you have discovered in your divorce journey.

- The adjustment to new role changes that have resulted from the divorce.

- The acknowledgment that the pain of loss is an inherent part of life resulting from the ability to give and receive love.

- A renewed sense of energy and confidence.

- The capacity to surround yourself with things that are nurturing to you.

Integration emerges much in the same way grass grows. Usually we don't check our lawns daily to see if the grass is growing, but it does grow, and soon we come to realize it is time to mow the grass again. Likewise, we don't look at ourselves each day of our divorce transition and see how we are healing. Yet we do come to realize, over the course of months, that we have come a long way. We have taken some important steps toward integration.

Usually there is not one great moment of arrival, but instead subtle changes and small advancements. It helps to have gratitude for even very small steps forward. If you mustered the energy to meet your friend for lunch, be grateful. If you had a good night's sleep, rejoice.

Of course, you will take some steps backward from time to time, but that is to be expected. Keep believing in yourself. Set your intention to integrate this divorce into your life journey and have hope that you can and will go on to have renewed meaning and purpose in our life.

EXPRESS YOURSELF: Go to *The Transcending Divorce Journal*, p. 116.

Integration Means Living the Truth

True integration of divorce into your life demands embracing the truth; it means opening your heart and making peace with yourself and the world around you. You honor this life-changing experience by giving it the attention it deserves, releasing it to your past, and creating new direction for your life. The afterglow of divorce allows for learning, growth, development, and transitioning into a new phase of living. The key is to

"We know the truth, not only by reason, but also by the heart."

Blaise Pascal

be able to look back on your marriage as another phase of life, not as a "failure." No, your marriage did not last a lifetime, but that reality by no means translates to a failure. Instead, you have entered into a new adventure that invites you to learn new skills, make mistakes and learn from them, cultivate new interests, and move in new directions.

So, healing from divorce involves...

...encountering what is most feared.

...opening to what it might be tempting to close yourself off from.

...a never-ending journey toward feeling wholeness.

...an honoring of your past as you hope for the future.

...a transformation of your heart and soul.

Yes, healing from divorce loss requires that we surrender to the energies of grief and descend into and through the painful experience. The reality is that we must plunge into the darkness before we can step into the light. In doing so, we create conditions that allow and encourage something new to arise within us. Yes, you can and will rise from the depths of your grief and discover unexpected healing and transformation. My hope is that in reading this book, using the companion journal and perhaps participating in a support group, you have affirmed that this healing occurs not by separating yourself from pain, but by attending to it.

Integration Means Being Congruent

Congruency is a term used in geometry. Congruent triangles coincide at all points when superimposed upon each other. This is a state of being in agreement, a state of corresponding.

Years ago, psychologist Carl Rogers created a model of human behavior based on the concept of congruency. He believed that to fulfill our purpose as human beings, we need to be congruent on three levels. The core level, our essence, needs to be congruent with our middle level, which is what we perceive ourselves to be. The surface level, our "form," consists of our behaviors and the self we display to the outside world. To be congruent, what we do and how we act on the surface level needs to match how we perceive ourselves and what is in our essence.

If you are living congruently, you:

- try to be honest at all times.

- are aware of who you really are and do not wear masks.

- honestly claim your thoughts and speak them.

- honestly claim your feelings and show them.

- honestly claim your mistakes and try to correct them.

- honestly claim your doubts and questions and raise them.

- honestly claim your beliefs and live them.

If you are living congruently, you are the genuine article. Congruence is about living from the inside out, being aware of your essence and living it. As the saying goes, what you see is what you get. If you have been existing in an unhappy marriage, usually you have not been able to live congruently. In my experience supporting many people, I have discovered that when we do our emotional and spiritual work surrounding divorce, we are able to live more authentically from the inside out. And, I ask you, what could be better than that?

> *"Honesty is the first chapter in the book of wisdom."*
>
> Thomas Jefferson

EXPRESS YOURSELF: Go to *The Transcending Divorce Journal*, p. 117.

Integration Means Being Self-Responsible, Yet Patient

Movement towards healing can be very draining and exhausting. Remember to seek out people who give you hope for your healing and believe in your capacity to integrate this divorce into your life. The right friendships provide a trail marker of stability in difficult times. Permitting yourself to have hope is central to achieving integration.

The hope that comes from the journey through your divorce transition is new life. The most important word in the previous sentence is *through*. As you do your emotional and spiritual work, you do not remain where you are; instead, you perturbate!

Yes, at times, darkness may have seemed to surround you. But rising up within you is the profound awareness that the pain that comes with divorce is a sign of having given and received love. And where the capacity to love and be loved has been before, it can be again. Choose new life!

Living in the present moment of your divorce journey (surrendering to where you are at this moment in time) while having hope for a good that is yet to come are not mutually exclusive. Actually, hoping and even anticipating can deepen your experience of the moment, and motivate you to keep doing your work!

Realistically, even though you have hope for your healing, you should not expect it to happen overnight. Many people want an instant resolution, not integration and transformation. Many people want to go around the wilderness instead of through it. But whenever we try to shorten our emotional and spiritual experience of pain and loss, we actually lengthen it. As the old maxim says, "The longest distance between any two points can be the shortest." I have seen many people in counseling who are in pain not because their relationship ended, but because they prolonged their pain by

> *"The keys to patience are acceptance and faith. Accept things as they are, and look realistically at the world around you. Have faith in yourself and in the direction you have chosen."*
>
> Ralph Marston

trying to avoid, deny, or go around it.

So, when it comes to time and healing, don't confuse efficiency with effectiveness. One of my mantras is "no rewards for speed." Don't try to cheat or rush the wilderness experience, or you won't come to a true integration. While it is instinctive to want to rush to resolution in this hurried culture we live in, I urge you to be patient and perturbate toward authentic integration.

You may find it helpful to take inventory of your own timetable and expectations for integrating this loss into your life. Ask yourself questions like, "Am I expecting myself to heal more quickly than is humanly possible? Have I mistakenly given myself a specific deadline for when I should be "over" my divorce?" Recognize that you may be hindering your own healing by expecting too much of yourself. Take your healing one day at a time. It will ultimately allow you to move toward and rediscover continued meaning in your life.

EXPRESS YOURSELF: Go to *The Transcending Divorce Journal*, p. 117.

Counsel from Rainer Maria Rilke on the Value of Patience

"Be patient toward all that is unsolved in your heart and try to love the questions themselves, like locked rooms and like books that are now written in a very foreign tongue. Do not now seek the answers, which cannot be given you because you would not be able to live them. And the point is to live everything. Live the questions now. Perhaps you will then gradually, without noticing it, live along some distant day into the answer."

Hope and Faith as Trust

In the Introduction to this book, I defined hope as "an expectation of a good that is yet to be." So, living with hope in the midst of your divorce is living with anticipation that you can and will go on to discover a continued life that has meaning and purpose. If you are in any way like I was when I went through my divorce, you may sometimes lose hope and need to fall back on your faith.

Sometimes in my own divorce journey, when hope seemed absent, I opened my heart—my well of reception—and found that it was faith that sustained me. Faith that was inspired by moments when I was able to find what was good, what was sweet, what was tender in life, despite the deep, overwhelming wounds of my grief. It was courage of the human spirit, which invites us to live fully until we die, that gave me faith. Life will continue, and it will bring you back to hope. If you lose hope along your journey, I invite you to join me in falling back or falling forward on faith.

Reflect on this: Living with hope is living in anticipation of what can be. Sometimes when we are in the wilderness of divorce, it is easy to question our hope for the future. But living with faith is embracing what cannot be changed by our wills and knowing that life in all of its fullness is still good.

Hope and Faith in God

In the religious traditions of Christianity and Judaism, hope is much more than an expectation of a good that is yet to be. Hope is knowing that God is partnering with you. And, with God as your partner, you are in pretty good company. Hope is knowing that you are being divinely guided, even during challenging times like divorce. Hope is believing that God may well send you a message or reassurance when you need it the very most. Hope is trust in God, even when everything seems hopeless. Hope is choosing to see the world around you through a lens of gratitude. Hope is looking for the gifts you received in your marriage. Hope is the assurance that God has the last word, and that word is life, even as you confront the realities of divorce. Yes, choose new life!

EXPRESS YOURSELF: Go to *The Transcending Divorce Journal*, p. 118.

A Final Word About Integration

When I reflect on integrating divorce into your life, I think of choosing to make life good again. That is the essence of integration—to make your life good again. You have the capacity to accomplish this. Through setting your intention to heal, nurturing yourself, and reaching out for help from others, you can and will make your life good again.

In fact, in some ways, your new life might be more than good. It might be richer and more deeply lived. This transformative power of divorce transition is the subject of the tenth and final Touchstone.

Touchstone Ten

Appreciate Your Transformation

"Transformation in the world happens when people are healed and start investing in other people."

Michael W. Smith

The journey through divorce is life changing. When you leave the wilderness of your experience, you are simply not the same person as you were when you entered the wilderness. You have been through so much. How could you be the same?

I'm certain you have discovered that you have been transformed by your divorce journey. Transformation literally means an entire change in form. Many divorced people have said to me, "I have grown from this experience. I am a different person." You are indeed different now. Your inner form has changed. You have likely grown in your wisdom, in your understanding, in your compassion.

Now, don't take this the wrong way. Believe me, I understand that the growth resulted from something you would have preferred to avoid. Though divorce can indeed transform into growth, neither you nor I would seek out the loss of a significant marriage relationship in an effort to experience that growth.

Let me assure you that this book is not about advocating divorce as a means to growth, even though growth is often the result. It is about helping you do your mourning of lost dreams and helping you move toward a new, satisfying and meaningful life. Yes, while divorce can be the end of a dream, it can also be a new beginning. If a divorce is going to happen, let's make it a transformative time of renewal, not a time of useless regret. For many of us, once the initial venture into the wilderness has taken place, and our pain has been befriended, divorce can be liberating. I certainly know it was for me.

"If we can recognize that change and uncertainty are basic principles, we can greet the future and the transformation we are undergoing with the understanding that we do not know enough to be pessimistic."

Hazel Henderson

While I have come to believe that our greatest gifts often come from our wounds, these are not wounds we masochistically go looking for. When others offer untimely comments like, "You'll grow from this," your right to be hurt, angry, or deeply sad is taken away from you. It's as if these people are saying you should be grateful for the divorce. Of course you're not grateful for the divorce. However, you may feel relieved if the stresses and demands of coping with a troubled marriage are no longer an issue. In addition, it is human to not miss the put-downs and hostility that sometimes accompany the end of a difficult relationship. But again, "grateful" is usually not the right word to describe your feelings.

The good news is that the bulk of women and men who go through a divorce do survive the upheaval of the marriage breakup and go on to create new and satisfying lives. Divorce can open an opportunity for a fresh start, for the creation of new dreams, and for an authentic and congruent life.

Divorce often frees good people from marriages that have been filled with unhappiness and dissatisfaction. Many people blossom in this new period of rediscovery of self. In many ways, you are forced to grow up! You are invited to learn and develop in ways that can result in happiness and joy entering your life. You have a new chance at life. Your self-esteem may improve and with it, your overall sense of life satisfaction.

Divorce brings the freedom to explore pathways of change that you may have previously considered, but didn't think were possible. You have the opportunity to learn new and more effective ways to manage the cognitive, physical, emotional and spiritual aspects

"Sometimes a breakdown can be the beginning of a kind of breakthrough, a way of living in advance through a trauma that prepares you for a future of radical transformation."

Cherrie Moraga

of your life. You have the opportunity to enjoy the support of old friends and create new friends. You have the opportunity to climb to the top of a peak instead of staying down in the bottom of a valley.

Yes, divorce is a transition that teaches us more than we may have imagined possible. And, most of us who make it through this wilderness experience see ourselves as true survivors. We know something about life now that we may not have known before. We can get more out of it. And, perhaps, even more important, we discover how to give more, too!

EXPRESS YOURSELF: Go to *The Transcending Divorce Journal*, p. 122.

Potential Growth: Growth Means More...

To understand how transformation from divorce might occur in your life, let's explore some potential aspects of growth:

- Growth Means More *Meaning and Purpose*
  As you integrate your divorce into your life, your conscious mourning of lost dreams of the relationship invites questions like, "Who am I?" and "What am I meant to do with my life?" "Does my life really matter?" Going through a divorce puts you face-to-face with the big questions of life.

Divorce seems to make us crave meaning and purpose in our everyday actions. Meaning is defined by intention and significance. Living life with meaning is the very opposite of just going through the motions of living. Giving attention to your divorce experience has a way of transforming your assumptions, values and priorities. You may now value material goods and financial status less and friendships more.

In a very real sense, divorce sets you on a path that involves a search of the soul. You may begin to ask another question, where do I look to discover myself? Paradoxically, as you acknowledge your divorce outside of yourself, you begin to look inside. Purpose is already within us, just waiting to be discovered.

If you open yourself to what is inside, you will find it. Once you have discovered it, you will be invited to live it. To go inside and explore your life purpose can be a frightening experience. After all, the journey on the inside is risky. You might feel lost and alone. You might be afraid of what you will find. You might worry that you will have to make some more significant life changes.

In part, purpose means living inside the question, "How can I discover my purpose for being in this world and fulfill that purpose?" Beyond that, it means being able to be a vital part of the universe, in harmony with something larger than yourself.

> "The purpose of life is a life of purpose."
> Robert Byrne

In many ways, divorce seems to free the potential within to discover your gifts and put them to use in the world. Helping others in some way, shape or form is, for many people who go through divorce, a vital part of discovering gifts and putting them to use. So, ask yourself, how can I help my fellow human beings? What are the gifts I have that will help me to help others?

Purpose helps define our contributions to life. It may find expression through friendships, family, community, work and spiritual concerns and acts. You may become aware that you are already fulfilling your destiny.

Living on purpose can be a way of life, a discipline to be practiced every day. It mandates a real desire to face each new day with the question, "Why did I get out of bed this morning?" The good sense to ask and the boldness to answer this critical question forms the centerpiece of living on purpose.

EXPRESS YOURSELF: Go to *The Transcending Divorce Journal*, p. 123.

• Growth Means More *Energy and Life Force*
When you integrate your divorce into your life, you unleash your inner power and divine spark—that which gives depth and purpose to your living. When you experience integration, you have more energy and enthusiasm for living. Not only do you have greater stamina, you also emanate vitality. You radiate positive energy and engage in life in ways that connect you to the greater world of humanity.

Life is the basic force that animates us. When you integrate your divorce, it is as if you can wake up to life and experience more of it. Your senses become more acute and you become more open and engaged in what is going on around you. You feel alive, vibrant and vital.

Now you can engage fully in life. Instead of letting life just happen to you, now you understand more, and your enhanced awareness unleashes energy to create your own destiny. Now you are not just existing, you are living abundantly.

EXPRESS YOURSELF: Go to *The Transcending Divorce Journal*, p. 123.

• Growth Means More *Feelings*
When you integrate your divorce into your life, you can experience your feelings more openly, honestly, and deeply. You are able to feel a full range of emotions, from sadness, protest, and anxiety to love, joy, and passion. You become more authentic and alive.

Sometimes when you are in an unfullfilling marriage, you

disengage from life by withdrawing or hyper-living. This disengagement can result in a lack of awareness of not only your own feelings, but other people's feelings as well.

When you have masked feelings, you live with a false self—a life out of touch with feelings that can guide you. By contrast, when you become more conscious of your feelings, you begin to honor them and trust them. Learning to befriend your feelings allows you to become more expressive of your real self. The happy consequence is greater intimacy with yourself and others. Now, instead of being "checked out," you are "checked in!"

EXPRESS YOURSELF: Go to *The Transcending Divorce Journal*, p. 123.

• Growth Means More *Love, Intimacy and Connection*
  In becoming your congruent self, you come to know yourself more fully, and others come to know you as well. You can now open yourself up. You can now allow yourself to be vulnerable and allow love in.

Mourning your lost marriage relationship well now makes it possible to love well in the future. (WARNING: Be patient and wait until you step out of the deep, dark wilderness and experience the light of integration before you begin a new relationship.) You become a person you respect and value. Experiencing self-love allows you to receive the love you now open your heart to. You make yourself available and emanate a desire to connect deeply and intimately to those around you.

> *"Love is the only thing we can't live without."*
> A.D.W.

In opening your broken heart, you open yourself to the rebirth of living and loving until you die. We all need love in our lives. Many of us eventually seek love after a divorce transition because we come to realize that love is the only thing we can't live without. In every breath you take, you can and will come to know this truth. No matter what else you pursue in life, love is always your most passionate and important quest. Love is the substance and essence of life. Opening your heart wide allows you to recognize that love is the foundation of your new life of passion and true joy. Now you can have more life, more meaning and more love than you ever imagined possible.

EXPRESS YOURSELF: Go to *The Transcending Divorce Journal*, p. 124.

• Growth Means More *Possibilities*
The integration of your divorce into your life opens you to a multitude of options. You may well discover an inner calling that invites you to follow your dreams. What have you always wanted to do but never did? What have you always told yourself was impossible? All that seemed impossible is now possible.

EXPRESS YOURSELF: Go to *The Transcending Divorce Journal*, p. 124.

• Growth Means More *Quality of Experience*
Your everyday activities become more purposeful as you achieve integration of your divorce transition. You understand more about why you do what you do each moment of your life. You feel deeper meaning in your living and have increased insight into why you think and feel the way you do.

EXPRESS YOURSELF: Go to *The Transcending Divorce Journal*, p. 124.

• Growth Means More *Satisfaction and Fulfillment*
Doing your divorce work allows you to discover your talents and gifts. By developing yourself and embracing your gifts, you feel fulfilled and one with the world around you. As you project a spiritual optimism into the world, you experience true satisfaction in living your life.

EXPRESS YOURSELF: Go to *The Transcending Divorce Journal*, p. 125.

• Growth Means More *Truth*
Making peace with your divorce invites you to live the truth.

Living the truth is itself a journey into self-reflection and discovery. To live in truth is to be conscious that your truth may not be now what it once was or what it will be in the future, but it is your obligation to live and speak your truth in the present moment. Integrating your divorce into your life encourages you to search for the truth inside you that has been longing to be expressed and to find the words to speak it. Surrender yourself to the truth, for to live your life in truth is to live in freedom.

EXPRESS YOURSELF: Go to *The Transcending Divorce Journal*, p. 125.

• Growth Means More *Faith and Spirituality*
As you integrate your divorce into your life, you feel gratitude for what you have in life. The heart of faith is believing you are not alone. And now you realize you are not alone. You can see that life is a sacred journey and come to trust in the goodness that surrounds you.

You may well discover that you have the opportunity to become a "spiritual gourmet." While a food gourmet knows how to put together wonderful menus, a spiritual gourmet learns how to put together a wonderful life. You can harmoniously meld life ingredients such as work, play and service—all surrounded in love.

EXPRESS YOURSELF: Go to *The Transcending Divorce Journal*, p. 125.

• Growth Means *Transcendence*
Have you noticed that though the title of this book is *Transcending Divorce*, we haven't yet fully explored what transcendence means? To transcend means to go above and beyond. It means to surpass and exceed.

Abraham Maslow, one of the founding fathers of modern psychology, said that human beings have a hierarchy of needs. According to Maslow, our bottom-level needs are physical, and include the need for food, water and shelter to keep us alive.

Our highest-order needs are spiritual and include the need for transcendence. People who achieve transcendence are able to live lives of unconditional love, altruism and inner joy.

In transcending divorce, you find your higher self. As you emerge from the wilderness of your grief, you go above and beyond the life you have lived before and achieve a deeper understanding of the meaning and purpose of your life. You find self-fulfillment and realize your true potential.

Transformation and transcendence go hand-in-hand. As you transcend, you are transformed. As you are transformed, you transcend. Embrace your transcendence and revel in your transformation.

EXPRESS YOURSELF: Go to *The Transcending Divorce Journal*, p. 126.

Carrying Your Transformation Forward

In his wise and lovely book *Soul Mates*, Thomas Moore makes the following observation:

> The word divorce doesn't mean 'to end' or 'terminate';
> it means to turn away, to separate, or to be turned in
> different directions. Divorce and diversion are closely
> related, both coming from the Latin *divertire*. This
> etymology suggests that divorce is not a failure of
> the parties to maintain their commitments, but rather
> evidence of the tendency of fate to spin us in different
> directions. When our thoughts about endings are faced
> with moralistic judgment, we create a culture filled with
> guilt, fantasies of impossible perfection, and the wrong
> kind of responsibility. When we are loaded with guilt,
> it is impossible to be truly responsible. If, on the other
> hand, our thoughts of ending were colored by genuine
> piety and an acknowledgment of life's centrifugal forces,
> then without overlooking the pain, we might also see the
> wisdom in a relationship's ending.

If you can accept the fact that endings such as divorce are woven into the basic fabric of our lives, you can impact your beliefs about divorce. Instead of

"Let yourself be silently drawn by the stronger pull of what you really love."
Rumi

seeing divorce as a failure of self and of society, you can accept it as the end of a relationship—a difficult, painful, yet survivable life transition.

Tomorrow is now. It is here. It is waiting for you. You have many choices in living the transcendence that healing from your divorce will bring to your life. Be open to the direction your life is now taking you. Listen to the wisdom of your inner voice and follow the guidance of your inner spirit. Make choices that are congruent with what you have learned on your journey.

Look for the graces that surround you. Remember that grace expands your intellect by gifting you with intuitive wisdom. You can now be guided by something you would not find through logic. Now you can

Grace: The knowing that you are not alone, that you are always accompanied. Grace expands your will by giving you courage you did not have before.

find your true life path and live through the pain that comes with the journey.

What are some of the additional signs that you have integrated your divorce transition into your life and that you have stepped out of the dark and into the light?

- You feel a sense of belonging in the world around you, as if the universe were embracing you.

- You experience a full sense of joy, of not being alone as you face things in life.

- You experience times when you feel you are in contact with your inner source of wisdom, love and healing.

- You notice a persistent sense that someone or something genuinely wants you to evolve and fulfill your potential. This comforting presence is supporting you without judgments or conditions.

- You feel mysteriously supported and loved at times when you need it, keeping you open to the divine.

- You persevere even in the face of adversity. You create goals for yourself and set about accomplishing them with continued, patient effort.

- You experience a loving presence in the universe that surrounds you. You can experience the feeling of being personally loved by the people in your life and you can express love to them.

- You experience a gentleness of spirit and kindness of heart. Gentleness eases the way and adds grace to your life. It softens your sorrows and cushions the burdens. Kindness becomes a natural virtue you express in the world. Your kindness soothes, calms, and renews you as well as the other souls your life touches. Kindness adds hope-filled texture to every aspect of your life.

- You experience the beauty around you. You come to realize that this moment, this day, this relationship, and this life are all unique, exquisite, and unrepeatable. There will be no moment exactly like this one. There will be no other day that unfolds precisely like the events and experiences of this day. You can now embrace every moment. You have gratitude that your entire life can be found in the timelessness of the moment you are in—right now.

- You experience gratitude for being more alive than you were in the past. You are aware your emotional and spiritual healing has transformed you and resulted in new energy in your body, nourishment in your mind, and illumination in your soul.

EXPRESS YOURSELF: Go to *The Transcending Divorce Journal*, p. 126.

My Prayer For You

May you continue to discover the freedom to live life with purpose and meaning every moment of each day. May you turn your face to the radiance of joy. May you live in the continued awareness that you are being cradled in love by a caring presence that never deserts you. May you keep your heart open wide and be receptive to what life brings you, both happy and sad. And, in doing so, may you create a pathway to living your life fully and on purpose until you die. Blessings to you as you continue your life journey toward wholeness. May your divine spark shine brightly as you share your gifts with the universe.

I hope we meet one day.

The Divorced Person's Bill of Rights

Though you should reach out to others on your journey through divorce, you should not feel obliged to accept unhelpful responses you may receive from some people. You are the one who is going through this naturally difficult experience, and as such, you have certain "rights" no one should try to take away from you.

The following list is intended to empower you to heal and decide how others can and cannot help. This is not to discourage you from reaching out to others for help, but rather to assist you in distinguishing useful responses from hurtful ones.

1. **You have the right to experience your own unique divorce journey.** While you will discover some commonalities with other people going through divorce, no one will have the exact experience you do. So, when you turn to others for help, don't allow them to tell you what you should or should not be feeling.

2. **You have the right to talk about your divorce experience.** Talking about this major life transition will help you integrate it into your life. Be selective, but do find people who are able and willing to listen to you as you move from head understanding to heart understanding of what you are experiencing.

3. **You have the right to feel a multitude of emotions.** It is important to befriend whatever feelings you are experiencing. Confusion, disorganization, fear, guilt, regret, sadness and relief are just a few of the emotions you might feel are a part of your divorce transition. Find listeners who will accept your feelings without condition.

4. **You have the right to be tolerant of your physical and emotional limits.** The divorce experience naturally leaves

you feeling fatigued. Respect what your body, mind and heart are telling you. Get daily rest. Eat balanced meals. And don't allow others to push you into things you don't feel ready to do.

5. **You have the right to experience "griefbursts."**
   Sometimes, out of nowhere, powerful feelings of sadness and loss may overcome you. This can be frightening, but it is normal and natural. Find someone who understands and will let you talk it out.

6. **You have the right to make use of ceremony.**
   A divorce ceremony does more than acknowledge the end of your marriage. It helps provide you with the support of caring people. Look for compassionate resources and people to help you plan and carry out a ceremony to mark your major life change.

7. **You have the right to embrace your spirituality.**
   If faith is a part of your life, express it in ways that seem appropriate to you. Allow yourself to be around people who understand and support your religious or spiritual beliefs.

8. **You have the right to search for meaning.**
   You may find yourself asking, "Why my marriage? Where did things go wrong? Will life be worth living again?" Some of your questions may have answers; some may not. Just remember—those who do not question do not find.

9. **You have the right to seek and accept support during and after your divorce.** You cannot—nor should you try to—go through this time of major change alone. Remember, you need not walk alone. Look for a compassionate companion to accompany you on this difficult journey.

10. **You have the right to be transformed by your divorce.**
    Transformation means an entire change in form. You are indeed different now. You have likely grown in your wisdom, in your understanding, and in your compassion. As you integrate your divorce into your life, you will feel gratitude for your life.

Acknowledgments

In my years as a counselor and educator, I have had the privilege of walking with many people journeying through the wilderness of divorce. They have shared their lives and intimate stories of love and loss with me. Without them this book would not be, nor would I be who I am. I want to thank every woman and man who was willing to talk honestly and openly with me about the divorce experience. It is through these people that these pages unfolded. While they remain nameless to preserve their privacy, each one of you has my gratitude and appreciation. Thank you for transforming your pain into wisdom and your sadness into joy.

I thank my colleagues at the Center for Loss and Life Transition. Kathy Anderson and Kerri LaFave help keep the Center focused on our vision of "helping people help others" during the natural challenges that come when I'm in exile writing a book. Your support, understanding, and friendship are invaluable to me.

To my colleague Raelynn Maloney for her willingness to read this book and make valuable suggestions for the content....a heartfelt thank you.

I have been gifted with an editor of exceptional insight and capacity for helping me express myself through the written word to my readers. Thank you, Karla Oceanak, for guiding my books into the light of the day.

To my family for the love and nurturance you provide to me each and every day. A special thank you to my precious daughter Jaimie, who brought me Advil and water when my hand cramped up from writing for long hours. She also took the lovely photographs of the grounds of the Center for Loss used in this book. She is an amazing 13-year-old young lady!

To contact Dr. Wolfelt and for information on his books and workshops, please write, call or e-mail:

Alan Wolfelt
Center for Loss and Life Transition
3735 Broken Bow Road
Fort Collins, CO 80526
970-226-6050
www.centerforloss.com

The Transcending Divorce Journal

Exploring the Ten Essential Touchstones

For many people, journaling is an excellent way to process the many painful thoughts and feelings after a divorce. While private and independent, journaling is still the outward expression of grief. And it is through the outward expression of grief that you heal.

ISBN 978-1-879651-54-8 • 150 pages • softcover • $14.95

The Transcending Divorce Support Group Guide

Guidance and Meeting Plans for Facilitators

When we are experiencing feelings of grief and loss during and after a divorce, we need the support and compassion of our fellow human beings. Divorce support groups provide an opportunity for this very healing kind of support.

ISBN 978-1-879651-56-2 • 64 pages • softcover • $12.95

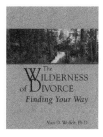

The Wilderness of Divorce

Finding Your Way

Divorce is a significant loss in life and must be mourned if the divorced person is to go on to love again. This hardcover gift book is a compassionate, easy-to-read guide to finding your way through the wilderness of divorce. This book is an excerpted version of the comprehensive *Transcending Divorce: Ten Essential Touchstones*, making it a more concise, friendly guide for the newly divorced.

ISBN 978-1-879651-53-1 • 128 pages • hardcover • $15.95